Indrani Bachan-Persad wor|
Indies. Soon after obtaining
Coventry University in the United Kingdom in 2013, her
dissertation, *Mediatized Political Campaigns: A Caribbean
Perspective,* was converted into a book and published in 2017.
Her Coventry experiences further inspired her to write this non-
fiction book of episodic events in her life. Soon after leaving
England, she was co-opted by the Government of Trinidad and
Tobago, to lead the communications thrust at two state boards.
Dr Bachan-Persad was the founding editor of The University of
the West Indies's first newspaper, *UWItoday*, and is a columnist
in one of the daily newspapers, writing on media and politics in
her country.

I dedicate this book to my family and dear friends who have supported my creative need to put pen to paper to write this book of short stories, during my period of study in Coventry. I thank you for your kind words of encouragement and support through this trip down memory lane.

Indrani Bachan-Persad

SUNLIGHT DANCING IN THE SNOW

AUSTIN MACAULEY PUBLISHERS™

LONDON • CAMBRIDGE • NEW YORK • SHARJAH

A CIP catalogue record for this title is available from the British Library.

ISBN 9781788485777 (Paperback)
ISBN 9781528901390 (ePub e-book)

www.austinmacauley.com

First Published (2020)
Austin Macauley Publishers Ltd
25 Canada Square
Canary Wharf
London
E14 5LQ

I wish to thank Coventry University for all courtesies extended during the three years I studied there, especially those who went out of their way to make my stay comfortable and happy including faculty at the School of Art and Design, staff at the International Office and the Pillar Box where I spent most of my short stays.

I also thank my family and close friends who took the time to visit me, as well as those, who supported me while I was there and from whom I have drawn inspiration in writing this memoir of my journey—Kassinath and Chelsea Persad, Poptee Bachan, Rhona Bachan, Angela Bachan-Khan, Carol Bachan, Tony Bachan, Rishi and Maria Mahabir, Nigel and Nicole Williams, Motilola Akinfemisoye, Fred and Florence Mudhai and Bhoendradatt Tewarie.

Thanks also to Beau Daniel, the talented artist who has worked with me on the creatives for this book, namely the black and white drawings depicting the essence of the stories.

I thank Coventry for being my home away from home during this period in my life and for inspiring me with its quaintness, mystery, medieval history and peaceful ambience.

Most of all, I thank God for giving me this rare opportunity in my life, to pursue my dreams and to achieve what I once considered impossible.

Table of Contents

Introduction

The year after I received my certification from Coventry University, I got up early one morning with thoughts of my experiences swimming in my head. Over the next few weeks, these thoughts consumed me and would not go away. It was like a movie as episode after episode played out in my head. I would go to bed thinking of my time there and get up with these thoughts fresh in my mind. In an attempt to quiet my thoughts, I decided to write them down. It was the easiest writings I have ever put on paper. The stories wrote themselves as they poured onto the paper, wanting to be heard, to take shape and form and I decided to give life to them. By the time I had got it all out of my system, it had miraculously formed into a book which I now share with my readers, for their enjoyment. These stories are very personal to me and I hope that it inspires others to follow their dreams.

To this day, I cannot truly understand or explain why I chose this remote town and university, way off in the midlands of the United Kingdom, to further my education. The name 'Coventry' held an uncanny attraction when I first heard it while working at The University of the West Indies, during a visit by two academics. At that time, it was still a relatively unknown university and many persons, especially those in academia, looked down their noses when I mentioned I was pursuing my doctoral studies there. It did not matter to me. It was the right place for me and I knew it as soon as I arrived there. I liked the quaint town, the many ancient cathedrals, the medieval fables attached to its name, the link to the rhymes which I grew up on as a child in primary school and the unusual circular shape of the town which seemed to always end up in the city square with the large statue of the fabled Lady Godiva bestride her horse.

I also liked that the university was located next to the ruins of the St Michaels Cathedral and that it was relatively small and spread out in the city centre, easy walking distance from any given point. Everything about the university and the city fascinated me, and in a way, it chose me rather than the other way around. Since when I first went there on official business, the idea of doing a PhD was the furthest thing from my mind.

Over the four years I was there, Coventry was very good to me. It provided the sanctuary I needed, during a transitional time in my life. There was an unexplainable connection between Coventry and myself which I never understood, and if I ever chose to live abroad, this would be the place for me. When my period of study came to an end, I felt a deep sense of sadness knowing that I would not be going back there again. I feared that the connection I had to this place might be lost. It was not to be. Almost annually since then, I would find a reason to revisit this place I had grown to love and I realised my connection to this quaint town far transcended the one I had with the university.

I write this book therefore as a memoir of my journeys to Coventry and the other places in Europe which I was fortunate to visit while studying there. Most of all, I hope that the book pays tribute to a place which I held close to my heart and continue to do so this day. This is my story.

My Journey to Coventry

By the time I started working at The University of the West Indies, I had already completed a full career in the public service; having worked with three different regimes, over a decade in the public service as a public relations officer in the Government Information Division. Over the time I spent there, I was fortunate to work with a number of government ministries such as Trade and Industry, Foreign Affairs, Consumer Affairs and Social Development. This job propelled me in the frontline as one of my main tasks was to be an intermediary between government ministers and the media. This job wetted my appetite for politics and deepened my interest in the local media. I was especially fascinated by the transition of fresh-faced ministers who took office with much fanfare and enthusiasm only to see the jaded look of disappointment over time.

As I sat ritualistically each week in the media room with the press, listening to the endless debates in the Senate and Parliament of Trinidad and Tobago, I grew to appreciate the local media and the work which they performed, and the challenges of meeting their deadlines to get their story to press on time. During this time, an easy camaraderie developed between us in the state media and those in the private media, each appreciating the respective roles we had to play in disseminating information to the wider public about the government's plans and policies.

However, this job made me aware of the challenges and dangers of putting yourself up for politics in a small country like Trinidad and Tobago. One of the main jobs of information officers was to attend weekly parliamentary and senate meetings in the 'Red House', the official Parliament of

Trinidad and Tobago. In 1990, when the democratically elected government, National Alliance for Reconstruction was overthrown in the Parliament by the radical Muslim group, the Jamaat-al-Muslimeen, I was attending my sister's wedding in Canada. At that time, I thought how lucky I was to be on vacation and not be assigned to cover Parliament that day.

Although, over the years, I had begun to grow weary of the job I was doing. I was hesitant to work in St Augustine because I felt that it was too remote from Port of Spain, where I had grown accustomed to the hustle and bustle of the capital city. When I was interviewed for the job, one of the panellists sitting around the sombre conference table, looked me up and down as if I were a specimen on a table and asked if I would be comfortable talking to professors and other esteemed pedigreed academics at the university. At the time, I thought what an odd thing to ask, given by background working with three regimes of government and countless Ministers of Government whom I had easy access to on a daily basis. My job in government communications was the most badly paid job but was one of the most exciting ones I held, taking me to all parts of the country and meeting with all types of people, from the big businessman in high powered meetings, to the ordinary folks in rural parts of the country, planting their gardens or going out to sea to catch fish to sell in the market. I had colleagues who had become good friends, some of whom moved on to politics and actually graced the house of parliament. As I stood there before the panel, I wondered if I was making the right decision and whether I was ready to transition to academia in St Augustine; a sleepy world of bespectacled professors and lecturers and unending and countless books as I perceived life on campus then.

When I assumed office, I was placed in a huge office in the Office of the Campus Principal. As I sat in my small desk at the far end of the office, I felt lost in that huge space with its high ceiling and intimidating walls. I discovered that the beautiful, white, colonial building, with its shuttered windows left open to let in the cool breezes from outside, was the official residence of former campus principals, and that my office was a recently converted bedroom. I loved the varnished wooden floors which led to an open area to the back of the building, with steps leading to a large expanse of lush, green grass, populated with exotic trees with names I did not recognise. This room, I was told, was the main family area or the great hall with an outdoor gallery overlooking the beautiful grounds and from where you could get a good view of the hills and Mount St Benedictine monastery, perched high atop the mountains.

The beauty and tranquillity of the building did not stop the aloneness I felt sitting in that huge room with the large wooden door shut to the outside world and the deadly silence which followed. I was happy that the large, glassed windows next to my desk allowed me to see the beautiful, landscaped grounds on the outside and the water fountain with its sprays of water shooting up in the air and gently cascading down the rock garden. From my desk, I could also see streams of bright-eyed students walking along the narrow road, just outside the office and the visitors exiting their cars as they made their way into the building for meetings.

From there, I was able to see the blaze of yellow flowers which completely covered the poui tree and formed a yellow canopy on the ground, during the summer periods. Also, within eyesight from my window was a pink-flowered tree, whose branches almost covered the entire area next to the fountain. One day, as I looked admiringly from my window, I noticed that the tree seemed to suddenly come alive; thinking it was just my vivid imagination, I scrutinised the tree a little closer, only to realise that the entire tree was covered with large red and black caterpillars. As a child, I had a phobia for these caterpillars which fed on the flowers in my mother's garden and which had me scampering in fear every time they settled there. Although, I was separated from these creatures by the glassed window, I still could not ease my fear and I felt shivers all over my body. Quickly, I grabbed the curtain rod, yanking hard to pull the thick drapes across the window, hoping to shut out these ghastly creatures and remove them from my eyesight. During the years I worked there, I refused to walk under that pink flowered tree, fearing that there might be caterpillars lurking in unseen parts of the tree, just waiting to fall on me. Other strange creatures also lived there and it was not unusual to see large black and white snails next to the fence by my office or the large, green iguanas walking lazily across the green grass, like it was nobody's business.

My introduction to UWI life was by no means an easy one. I had begun my career at the same time when a new principal was installed, and in some ways, I felt the brunt of an institution transitioning from one leadership regime to another. I was entrusted with the responsibility of stakeholder and media relations and over time, my duties were expanded to include varied projects as I settled down to work in this new environment. In due course, my portfolio was expanded to include coordinator of the International Office, a job which put me in touch with both international and local students. It was a job which I truly enjoyed. I loved working with the students, organising student exchanges and study abroad opportunities and meeting new faculty from international universities. It was through this job that I had my first introduction to Coventry and the world that was about to unfold for me, allowing me to broaden my view of the small country we live in.

One day, I was informed that some unexpected guests from a foreign university had arrived and I was expected to attend a meeting with them. As soon as I was introduced to the two gentlemen, I was enthralled by their university's quaint name 'Coventry'. Immediately, I recalled the saying 'Banished to Coventry' which I thought was a fabled place in a storybook which I had read as a child. I was reassured that the place actually existed in the midlands in England and was only accessible by bus. As part of the formalities of the meeting, an invitation was offered to visit at a convenient time. Over time, I forgot about Coventry as I went about my daily duties. However, the opportunity to visit came unexpectedly one day while planning an institutional visit to the United Kingdom, for a university contingent.

Remembering the open invitation to visit Coventry, I slipped it into the agenda and was elated when it was approved by the authorities.

Up to this time, even though I had developed a deep interest in media and politics, addictively perusing the pages of the newspapers daily, gobbling up all news and information on the media while doing my job at The University of the West Indies. I still did not have any intentions to pursue my doctoral studies after completing my graduate studies at the Arthur Lok Jack Graduate School of Business. I was happy and comfortable in my current job since I was assigned varied tasks which kept me busy and deeply interested as I became more integrated into university life. It was a time for me to learn, grow and acquire new skills, which I welcomed as part of my own self-development.

We never know why things happen the way they do and, in a way, in hindsight, I felt that there was a guiding hand which led me to these two visitors and my first introduction to Coventry and the fascination with the name, place, people which eventually opened a whole new life for me there. When I went to Coventry for the first time, I immediately felt the connection and it drew me like a moth to the light. My intuition was right and I was not disappointed. My journey to Coventry changed me considerably. I grew to appreciate Trinidad and Tobago more as I listened to the experiences of some of my foreign colleagues studying there. I began to discover things about myself which surprised me, such as my love for writing. In many ways, finding Coventry was akin to finding myself. From Coventry, I was able to explore other parts of Europe and learn about new peoples and cultures and broaden my perspective of the world.

Beginning of Something New

From as far back as I could remember, I dreamed of studying abroad. So, when the opportunity came unexpectedly, I was exhilarated at the prospect of being able to make this dream a reality. To determine whether this was really something that I could do, I journeyed to Coventry University in the heart of England twice, and within a short time, I was preparing to embark on this journey in my life. At that time, Coventry University was a relatively unknown small university in the Midlands which had started as a polytechnic institute, and in time was transformed into a fully accredited university.

The trip to Coventry entailed an extra hour and half train ride from London to the Midlands. My colleagues and I had to catch the early train, one cold, foggy morning, during peak rush hour. As we hastened to the underground, my colleagues headed off quickly in the direction of the train, and in the blink of an eye, disappeared in the underground. Not familiar with the train lines, panic quickly set in. One of them had all the train tickets to Coventry in their pocket and being unfamiliar with the train system, I quickly became confused. I reached into my coat pockets for my phone only to discover that there was no signal in the underground. As I looked around, not sure what to do, and with panic setting in, I felt a hand reach out asking if I was okay. It was a uniformed man, maybe a security guard who was possibly monitoring the underground from some hidden camera and realised that all was not well. I explained my dilemma and he immediately pointed to a spot close by where I could get a signal. I thanked him and headed to the spot, hoping that I would reach my colleagues in the station. I was relieved when I heard a concerned voice on the phone and was directed to board the next train and to get off at the designated Euston Station. I was both happy and angry at the same time to meet up with them. I did not speak for the entire train ride, and the party maintained a stony silence, glancing at me from time to time, perhaps in the hope that I would snap out of my bad mood.

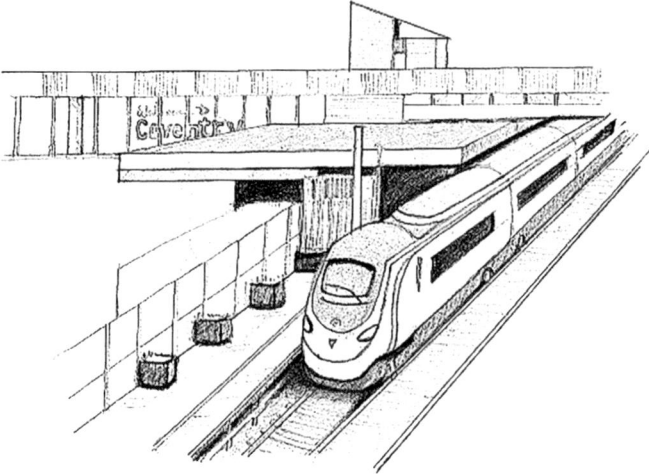

To get there we had to take a train from London, and even then, on the ride over, I marvelled at the large expanse of undulating meadows which reminded me of the Caroni plains in Tableland, a small village in rural Trinidad, not far from where I was born. It also reminded me of my early childhood days, attending primary school and reciting poems such as *Little Bo Peep* under the big seaman tree behind my mother's little wooden house, which was next to the school. I could almost see myself running through these meadows with its flock of sheep and my hair blowing in the wind…it never occurred to me how far-fetched that dream was to my current reality, a child of the country in rural Trinidad where meadows were really forests inhabited by animals, especially poisonous snakes which I feared with my life. Such were the dreams of a young country girl, reared on stories and poems written mostly by English authors and poets, and which were very much part of our colonial education.

When we arrived at Coventry, we were greeted by a faculty member who had met us in Trinidad. It was during that visit that I discovered that at a reasonable cost, I could undertake my postgraduate studies in my particular field, at minimal inconvenience to me and my family, while still working too! I was astounded, since never before did I think this could be possible. For the rest of our visit there, I played with the idea in my mind while we conducted our business. Still undecided, the following year, on another official visit to the United Kingdom, I journeyed to Coventry to speak with a faculty member there. He was very surprised that I had journeyed all the way there, to speak to him before enrolling for my graduate studies. It was because of this academic's reassurance and advice that my mind was finally made up and I enrolled in the university.

As a study-abroad member of staff from The University of the West Indies in the Caribbean, I was afforded a few extra curtsies and privileges, such as faculty housing with an extra room and a housekeeper who came in daily to take care of the place. These simple things made my life there comfortable and happy and I was truly grateful to the university for treating me with such respect and dignity. In the years to follow, I realised that because they were so student centred, they placed their students' comfort above all things. I was not surprised to see the rapid expansion and diverse student population over time, from all parts of the world.

I loved where I lived. The dorm was in the centre of the city, in the main shopping area. I enjoyed stepping out of the dorm, right into a store. Each day, I would visit the various stores, looking for bargains or simply browsing. I never got tired of shopping, even though most times I bought little or nothing. It kept myself busy and occupied. I especially loved the shops which sold colourful postcards of different shapes and sizes. Most times, I would return to my home country in December with packs of glossy Christmas cards, which I would proudly send to my friends and family. I was amazed how the British maintained some of their traditions such as, their love for reading, and in their bookshops one always found a number of persons browsing the many fully stacked shelves. During my period there, I too had reignited my love for reading and spent most of my Sundays curled up with a book in my bed, greedily eating up the pages for hours at a time. I loved reading historical novels and spent a good part of my free time reading about Coventry, the legend behind its name, the medieval connection and even the ghosts who lived there, according to some authors.

I also discovered that the English loved history much more than I did and they salvaged anything that they found from the past, be it churches, houses, streets and cemeteries with their slabs of mossy headstones with writings dating all the way back to the twelfth century. I loved walking past these places, reading the round, commemorative plaques placed on the walls of the buildings. In an area close to the Anglican Church, there were remnants of an ancient stone building next to a dug-up cemetery, with dark headstones lined up against the wall. I was truly amazed at the care and love with which this place was preserved, and loved walking on the cobbled street alongside the enclosed area, in the late afternoons. Next to this building was a huge monastery which appeared to be in rather good shape after all these years. I could visualise the many monks and nuns in their long habits, running around in that building, in centuries gone by. As I walked past the cemetery, I would usually stop briefly to admire the beautiful, large, stately English mansions, one of which once belonged to the mayor of Coventry. This building now housed students from the university.

Opposite the museum which was located within the university's compound and housed some ancient artefacts together with a pictorial recreation of the story of Godiva was an archaeological site of possibly the first and oldest castle in the town which was found during a routine excavation by workmen. I loved sitting quietly in the bench there, trying to imagine the type of life that existed there so long ago. Next to this site was one of the most magnificent buildings I had ever seen, the Council House. In days gone by, this was known as the Guildhall where the important men gathered to make important decisions about trade. I would occasionally walk up Bayley Street and sneak into the back entrance of the courtyard, looking up at the beautiful Victorian architecture in that old stately building. One day, I mustered up my courage to venture into the building and I silently walked through the many wooden floors with some of its original furniture, staring in awe at the paintings and artefacts in that great hall. On the day I visited, the hall was empty and as I walked noisily with my heavy boots, I felt that I was disturbing the ghosts who lived there. As I looked around, I suddenly became aware of the unnatural quietness of the hall and I began to get an uneasy feeling of being silently watched. Without much hesitation, I quickly exited the building, glad to feel the damp air on my cheeks.

During my first couple of years at Coventry University, I was given a study room all the way on the top floor of the Ellen Terry Building, which was once a cinema. Most of the times the lift did not work and I would find myself having to trek three flight of steps to get to the room. No easy task considering that the heavy layers of clothing during winter made this walk especially onerous. I hardly saw any students there and I felt quite uneasy sitting in that large room with no one around. One day, I was startled to hear a loud, piercing scream coming from outside. Quickly, I gathered my books and scampered out the room. As I walked down the stairs, the screams became louder and even more deafening. Curiously, I decided to follow the sound only to discover some undergraduate students were practicing for a school play. Eventually, I abandoned the room and ventured into the main library hoping to find a quiet space to study. On the contrary, I soon discovered that the library was the domain of undergraduates who never ceased to laugh, talk, eat or sleep there, and I was forced to retreat to the spooky room at the top floor of the Ellen Terry Building, once again. One day, I got a surprise visit from the Dean of the Faculty who must have sensed something was amiss. In my following visits to

Coventry. I was given a space in the faculty common room which was located in his office. I was happy for this because it allowed me to interact with faculty intermittently.

In my early period in Coventry, I spent much of my time alone, walking through the small town, admiring the historical buildings, visiting the shops, museum, market, churches and other sites. Sometimes, in the cold afternoons, I would take the short walk to the old church and sit quietly in one of the wooden chairs, away from everyone else deep in thought. Other days, I would sit eating alone in my favourite restaurant, watching students walking by, trying to guess where they came from. I cannot say I did anything special but during that early period, I found an immense sense of peace and happiness which I never really recaptured in my following visits.

My First Encounter
with the Godiva

When it was time to commence my studies, I arrived at Coventry University a week earlier than I should have and found out that they were not prepared for me. I stayed in an inexpensive hotel across the highway, at the opposite end of the university, while they got my room ready. Each morning, I would put on my shoes and my coat and go out exploring the surrounding areas. My daily treks enabled me to explore different parts of Coventry and to familiarise myself with the city.

On that August morning, soon after breakfast, I made my way to the town centre. I crossed over the busy highway, down another quaintly named 'Spon Street' with its fifteenth-century, timber-framed houses. I was to learn that the houses were brought there from other streets in the town, as a tourist attraction. I was fascinated by the shops with signs that indicated how old the buildings were and what they were currently being used for. One in particular had clocks from as many countries as I can remember with different times on them. Another was a butcher, and next to it a pub. Again, I wondered if I was in another era. There was something very comforting and safe about this place. Here, I was, a stranger in a foreign land and I felt safe as if I were in my home millions of miles away.

As I entered the town, through its ultra-modern designed mall, I marvelled at its glassed ceiling which shielded those beneath from the cold wintery English weather, but was like a mirror reflecting the skies above. I instinctively followed my nose and found a motley of small caravans selling an assortment of foods next to the large fountain at the city centre. With the winds having picked up, I immediately followed my nose and landed by the potatoes…baked potatoes with cottage cheese, topped with pineapple chunks became my favourite street food whenever I visited Coventry. It was the first place I stopped off for a meal, as soon as I arrived in Coventry. Although, I tasted the other foods sold in small caravans huddled in the square such as pork sandwiches, Chinese noodles, and German sausages… I always returned to the caravan with the hot baked potatoes and cottage cheese!

On my first trek across the highway, my eyes were drawn magnetically to the top of a tall church spire way up in the sky as far as the eye could see, a good distance away. The city itself seemed to be lifted out of one of Enid Blyton's storybook – the streets were narrow and winding, seeming to go up and then in a circular direction, just like the fairy tales I loved to read as a child, a world inhabited by mythical creatures such as gnomes, goblins, pixies, fairies and other magical creatures. Living in a remote part of the country, it was not too far-fetched for my fertile imagination to conjure up these fairy tales and convert the forested landscape into an English countryside, with its rolling plains covered with a canopy of lush green grass. It was my early love for books and the escape it offered which made me into an avid reader who gobbled anything on paper, especially stories which stirred my vivid imagination. Later on, I would read for a degree in literature and English at The University of the West Indies in my home country, losing myself in the pages of fiction by famous English authors and poets.

The city itself was like a circle, everything seemed to be leading to the centre with a huge, majestic statue of a magnificent naked lady bestride a horse with her long hair adorning her body. In a daze, I stared at the statue and wondered who she was. At the first opportunity, I bought a book on the history of the town and was pleasantly surprised that there was a whole fable concerning the 'Lady Godiva', as she was called. She was a wealthy benefactor who lived there with her husband, Leofric, in the twelfth century and both were known for their generosity to the ordinary people who were their subjects. As the fable goes, her husband wanted to raise the taxes of the city. The generous and kind-hearted woman, pleaded with him not do so and mockingly, he agreed. Only if she rode through the town naked and returned, would he grant her wishes. Being an adventurous soul and one not to be daunted, she ordered all the people of the town to shut their windows and decked only with her long, blond hair wrapped around her. She was led by her lady in waiting, through the town on her white mare. Rumour has it, that Tom, one of the town's men was so enamoured with her beauty that he could not help himself and peeped through a crack in the window and was immediately blinded by her beauty. It is said that her husband, being a man of his word, was so amazed at her audacity that he agreed to withhold the taxes from the townspeople.

For someone like me who grew up on nursery rhymes such as *Tom, Tom, the Peeping Tom*, I could not believe that an actual place existed where this fabled Tom once resided. In keeping with the theme, a small head depicting that of Tom's was placed on one of the arches of a building which surrounded the town square, close to the Lady Godiva statue. Each day, when I passed under the arched building, I could not help but look up at the face of Tom which was looking directly at the Lady Godiva statue in the square.

Godiva would have been 57 years old when her husband died. It is said that her body is buried in Coventry next to her husband and son but no one seems to know the exact location, and each time I passed by the cemetery in the churchyard, I could not help but wonder if she was there, looking at me instead and wondering why this stranger was walking in her land!

It is said that when Lady Godiva died, she decreed that the jewelled rosary which she wore should be placed around the neck of the Virgin Mary in Coventry Priory.

For the four years I studied there, this legend continued to fascinate me. I spent many hours reading books on the town and perusing the small museum in the university with the hope that I could fully understand her story – so much was my fascination and amazement at a woman who over a hundred years ago seemed to live on in the memories of a little town in a remote part of England, so much so that she has been placed majestically in the centre of the town, as a witness and perhaps a guard to her beloved people.

As I became familiar with life in Coventry, I developed my own routine. I still knew few people and over the years, preferred the solace of my own company rather than the chatter of strangers, especially students with their many accents. My routine was simple, early breakfast, a brisk walk though St Michael's Cathedral as I headed to the university to work for most of the day. In the afternoons, I would return to the city centre, spending a short time browsing into windows before returning to the dorm to settle down for the rest of the night.

This was a very satisfying period of my time there, and I relished the quiet retreat which Coventry allowed me, to reflect quietly on my life and studies there.

Following the Steeple in the Sky

As I walked in the direction of the church steeple, I stumbled upon the most marvellous structure I had ever laid my eyes upon – sitting like an old, wrinkled grandmother, protectively looking out at the university was the remnants of St Michael's Cathedral, which dates from 1300 AD and was one of the largest medieval parish churches of England. In 1249, the chapel was constituted into a church with the tower, octagon and spire dating from 1400 to 1450.

As I walked into the cathedral, I gazed at the steeple which led me there and as my eyes travelled upwards, I felt that I had just flown into the sky and was able to touch the clouds. Looking downwards, I felt like I was falling and held on to one of the wooden benches to steady myself. At the entrance of the church, my eyes alighted on the plain memorial stone dedicated to civilians killed in World War II. As I tried to decipher the reading on the stone, two tiny squirrels darted playfully between the green shrubs oblivious to my curious gaze.

As I walked into the church, I automatically registered all the details around me: the small statue of Christ looking protectively down at the cathedral; the beautiful Statue of Reconciliation which was gifted to the church by Sir Richard Branson; Jacob Epstein's Statue Ecce Homo whose meaning escaped me; the green effigy and tomb of Huyshe Yeatman-Biggs, the first Bishop of Coventry Cathedral; and the small mossy pews, or what was left of them on both sides of the church.

At the far end of church was a poster board with some barely discernible drawings pinned up on its wall. Instinctively, I walked over to the drawing, and realised it was a black and white pictorial depiction of how the church must have looked like before the unfortunate bombing during World War II. During the reconstruction of the cathedral, the town decided to keep the remnants of the old church and to build an entirely new church adjacent to it. It was a very wise decision and to this day, the church continues to attract many tourists from all over the world.

As I looked around at the uneven, hard, cobbled, stone floor; the windowless walls and roofless top lit by the natural sunlight peeping through the blue skies, I felt that there was something ethereal about this place and if I were to fathom a guess, I think that if God were to reside in this earthly world, this would be one of his homes. There was something so pure and untouched about this cathedral, even though it had been ravaged by war and grown old and mossy from the exposed elements and inclement weather.

As I walked towards the remnants of the pulpit at the front of the church, I felt an inexplicable emotion when my eyes alighted on a roughly hewed, wooden cross which seemed to have burnt marks on it, proudly standing in front of the shattered glass windows. I discovered that the wood for the cross was salvaged from two burnt beams that held the roof of the cathedral together and was built by stonemason Jack Forbes.

As I stood there in the cold, damp weather, silently surveying this wondrous place and its artefacts, I heard the ringing of bells echoing loudly from the church spire way above my head as if to welcome me into the church.

This Roman Catholic church was the centre of the town at a time when the church was one of the most important institutions of the land. Then, the town was mostly inhabited by monks and nuns and I can just imagine the dark-frocked pious ones attired in their habits, moving silently about in the conduct of their daily business, a scene I actually witnessed while visiting St John's University in the United States, years prior to this visit. It was a disturbing scene to see, the silent, dark frocked monks walking in a file which I never forgot.

During World War II, German leader, Adolph Hitler had decided to bomb this small industrial town, known for making watches and cars and had used its manufacturing skills to make canons and other artillery to fight against the Germans, in their war against Britain. On 14 November, 1940, the people of the town awoke to find their beautiful buildings smashed to pieces, their town completely destroyed by bombs dropped by German fighter jets in the middle of the night, including their cathedral which was completely burnt down.

The 295 feet church spire miraculously survived the blast from these huge bombs dropped from the sky, and I marvelled at how the city was able to rise like a phoenix from the ashes with little to show for the deadly blows which it dealt with at that time. I made it my duty to visit their museums and cathedrals each time I was there, so that I too would be inspired by these courageous people.

As I headed to the stairs to the side of the cathedral, I was able to survey the new church built from funds repatriated from the German government after the world war. From where I stood, the opaque glassed wall of the newly built church, enabled me to clearly see the modern design of the interior of the church with a peculiarly shaped depiction of Christ drawn in the entire wall behind the pulpit, forming a picturesque backdrop for the congregation to view during church services.

During my time in Coventry, this newly designed church did not hold the same attraction to me and I only entered its doors to attend my graduation ceremony, at the end of my studies. But the modern design, allowed those inside to get a good view of the old cathedral, while those on the steps where I stood could almost visualise themselves participating in the church service. It was a clever idea by the designer. The giant statue of Archangel Michael Angelo defeating the devil at the front of the newly built church was a stark, graphic reminder of the struggle and victory of the people of Coventry over a very dark period in their history.

As I surveyed the entrance to the main administration building of the university with its large, black cannon balls placed decoratively across the huge concrete pavilion, sprays of water jettisoned into the air falling elegantly back on the ground and disappearing miraculously into it. Smiling to myself, I turned around and headed back through the narrow alley between the two cathedrals, towards the city centre.

Taking the narrow-cobbled alley between the Holy Trinity Church and the restored archaeological site, I found myself passing a couple of beautifully Georgian designed houses, one of which once belonged Lord John Gulson, (1867–1868) the Mayor of Coventry. Further along, I found myself eye to eye with an ancient cemetery with its many dark, concrete slabs with dates and names too old to remember. Looking up from where I stood, I felt an eerie chill run down my spine, as I walked neck to neck with these ghastly tombs in the churchyard. Hastening my steps, within seconds, I found myself in front of Coventry's best-preserved historic buildings The Lych Gate Cottages which were aptly named after the lynch gate where carriages carried the coffins of departed ones, ready for burial in the parish cemetery. These beautifully black and white cottages reminiscent of the Victorian era were adjacent to the famed St Mary's Priory, founded by Earl Leofric and Lady Godiva.

The entire area seemed surreal and I felt like I had just returned to an Elizabethan or Victorian era, in which carriages were driven by well-dressed horsemen tipping their hats as they went by and ladies with their long-frilled frocks and beautifully decorated umbrellas enclosed by white laced, gloved fingers as they delicately took their afternoon walks. The juxtaposing of the magical, mystical, religious world of medieval Coventry with the modern-day town continued to mystify me each time I visited.

In my second year there, one of the shells from the bombs would be discovered underground late in the cold afternoon and I would marvel at the rapidity by which the town was cordoned off from the public, including myself who was coming out of the library to return to my room which was in the centre of the city. At that time, standing freezing in the fading light of that wintery afternoon with scores of confused foreign students and sirens blaring around us, the reality of my situation as a lone international student, far from home, with no one to turn to in times of crisis dawned on me. I was totally unprepared for this or any predicament which should befall me while studying there. Luckily, within an hour, it was discovered that the shell was not active and the yellow tapes were withdrawn just as quickly, and we were allowed to proceed with our business. I felt a tremendous sense of relief when I arrived at my accommodation in the city centre.

During the period I stayed in Coventry, I never got tired of the relics of the ancient St Michael's Cathedral which gave me a tremendous amount of peace, comfort and security. It was pivotal during my visits and as soon as I arrived there, I would make the small trek to the cathedral to say a few words of thanks and offer a small prayer.

Even to this day, whenever I think of Coventry, I also think of the magic of St Michael's Cathedral.

Accommodations, Cab Drivers and Food for Thought

Finally, after a week in the hotel, my hall of residence 'The Pillar Box' was ready. I taxied to the International Office to pick up my key late in the afternoon. I was handed a small electronic key fob and a taxi was called for my short trip to the hall of residence. With two suitcases, a laptop bag and hand luggage, I was expecting to be deposited at the entrance of the residence. Alas, this was not to be. The rude, arrogant cabdriver with the thick Indian accent, dropped both me and my bags unceremoniously at the back of the building, pointing in the direction of a long building spanning almost the whole length of the street and hastily drove off without even looking back. With no signs to indicate where I was, and left alone in the middle of nowhere with a number of bags late on that chilly afternoon, I was determined to find my room. Totally exasperated, I crossed the narrow lane behind the tall building and applied the fob to the only discernible door at the back of a long, unending building, not sure what to expect. After several attempts, the door swung open to a small empty foyer with steps leading to several floors above. As I dragged my bags in, I could not discern any lift, looking at the number on my key fob only to realise that I was on the top floor!

It dawned on me then that the cabdriver must have deliberately deposited me at the wrong end of the building in his haste to finish his workday and head home early. With much difficulty, I dragged one bag at a time across the narrow road, placing the key fob on the door in the hope that it would open. I was not to be disappointed as the glass door opened and I found myself in a small area at the bottom of a flight of stairs. Looking up exasperatedly, I began to slowly trek up the three flight of stairs, concluding that my room had to be on the third floor based on the number on the key fob. By the time I had deposited all three bags on the landing of the third floor, I was tired.

As luck would have it, a fellow student with a Nigerian accent happened to pass by and seeing my frustrated face quickly offered to assist me to my room. Immediately, she commandeered the last bag and dragged it up the stairs and without looking back, briskly strode down the corridor, in the direction of my presumed room. This good soul took me all the way to my room, which I discovered was really the entrance of the building. I still remember her gasp of amazement and awe when she opened the door for me. "You have a television and look how big your room is!" she exclaimed in amazement as if she had discovered a pot of gold at the end of a rainbow! As I peered tiredly into the room, I was not impressed, trying to understand what in this cold, drab room she found so amazing. I wondered for the first time what did I get myself into. I thanked the student and shut the door as I retreated into my small sanctuary which was to become my home for that semester.

The next morning, I was awakened by a sharp rap on my door. As I gingerly opened the door, I was greeted by a cherry faced, uniformed lady who warmly greeted me with a 'good morning' indicating that she had come to clean. As I opened the door, she entered and busily got to dusting and tidying the small room, chatting incessantly without expecting a response. It is from this good lady that I learnt the ins and outs of dorm life, and that there was a matron on the ground floor, in the room with the cameras that scanned all the floors of the dorm. In hindsight, I realised this was a precautionary measure for students who were accustomed to coming in all hours of the night, and for bringing in uninvited guests to stay. The dorm had a strict guest policy, however, as a faculty scholar, I was allowed to bring my family to stay with me in the visitor's accommodation where I was staying.

It was from her, I had a deep appreciation of the common folks in Coventry, having discovered that she awoke in the wee hours of the morning to come to work and left late in the afternoon after cleaning the entire building. Over time, I started to clean my own place, so as to ease some of her workload. She never complained but I think that she appreciated the help. She had one son whom she adored, and spent most of her money which she saved from her housekeeping job, going on vacation to places such as Malta and Greece.

Not for the first time, I thought how similar working-class people were across the world, including my own family who were descendants of Indian indentured labourers who came from India to work in the sugar plantations in the West Indian colonies. She never understood where Trinidad was, even though I tried to explain countless times. When I asked her if she knew about Jamaica, she nodded in the affirmative, and I indicated the proximity of my small country to that country to her. But it continuously amazed me that most British people never heard of my country and I had to find something or someone famous whom they knew, and through that association would make the connection to my country. Without fail, the names Brian Lara and Dwight Yorke, always did the trick, and for music lovers, I would only have to mention Bob Marley and their eyes would light up with recognition.

During my first year there, I also met three colleagues from China who were also pursuing their PhDs in similar areas. They were beautiful people, fashionably dressed with surprising English names. They had a difficult time since they did not speak English very well and I imagined that this posed some challenges in their studies. I discovered that they were all teachers in China and the Chinese government was paying for their education. They did not seem too worried about the language barrier and the impact on their studies, and I got the impression that they were just enjoying the freedom of living in a liberal country for a short period. By my second year, I did not see them and found out that they were struggling to keep up with their classes. However, one day while working in my office in Trinidad, I got an impassioned email from one of the girls desperately seeking my advice. I am not sure if they ever made it through and even though we exchanged emails, I lost touch with them altogether, as the years rolled by. I do believe that China's restrictions on internet access made it difficult for them to communicate with the outside world.

Over the years I was there, the number of Chinese students increased drastically in Coventry. My dorm where I usually stayed was now filled with mostly Asians. One afternoon, soon after arriving in Coventry, I opened my door to be welcomed by a pretty Chinese girl with a plate of cookies in hand, speaking in perfect English to me. Not too sure what to make of her, I politely declined shutting the door to her inquisitive eyes.

During my first internship, the weather had grown bitingly cold and during the night, I would layer piles of clothing on, including thick woollen socks while in bed. This did not help and one day, I walked into a Chinese massage shop, not too far away from where I was staying and after explaining my problem to the lady who spoke little English, was advised to do a special type of massage called 'cupping' which she promised will ease the excruciating pain. After a bit of coaxing and a short demonstration, I reluctantly agreed. As I laid down on my belly, awaiting the masseur to arrive, fear gripped me and I wondered if my spontaneity would land me in trouble. I must say, I wondered if my family would ever see me again. When the masseur came over with these lighted glass goblets and placed them, one at a time on my bare back, in the dimly lit room it felt pleasantly comforting, and gradually I relinquished my fear and relaxed on the small white bed. I did survive but it did not altogether stop the terrible pain in my bones, which continued for most of that semester. I must have developed immunity to the wintery English cold weather because over the years that pain disappeared without a trace. But I dare say, I was hesitant to do another round of cupping again.

The Pillar Box

On that particular night, I decided not to put on the regular layers of clothing as I nestled deep under the covers of my bed. I was suddenly jolted awake by a loud, shrill sound screeching endlessly in my ears. As I dazedly woke up, trying to identify the sound, I realised that an alarm in the building had gone off and the drill was to get out of the building at once. Fearing for my life, I grabbed the first thing in sight, my handbag as I slipped my cold feet into by bedroom slippers, scampering half-awake out of the room, into the smoke-filled corridor, behind lines of scantily dressed, sleepy-eyed students, unto the hallway and outside the building.

The splash of icy cold air woke us all fully at once. As I looked around, I was amazed at how many students from all parts of the world were standing shivering outside in the cold. I am sure that it ran through all our minds at how foolhardy we were since most of us neglected the most important thing – our coats! And I, being a true Trini, opted to grab my purse! I am not sure what I was thinking and as I watched the helmeted firemen run through the building with a long fire hose, shivering outside in this chilly dark night.

In less than an hour, the culprit was found – a burnt potato left by an errant student in the oven. Poor thing, probably fell asleep and the potato had burnt so badly that it had caused smoke to set off the alarm. I am not sure what had happened to the student after this. But a note was slipped under my door soon after the incident, indicating that students would be fined for any such acts and further for those students who did not leave their room when the alarm went off, they would also be fined in the future! Now why would anyone want to stay in an ancient building during a fire is anyone's guess.

In the following days, I discovered some quaint and memorable places such as the covered market selling an assortment of foods, clothing, books, suitcases and old memorabilia. I was fascinated by the variety of fresh vegetables especially the beautiful array of sweet peppers. I soon learnt the concept of 'a bowl', literally meaning a big plastic bowl like the one used in my kitchen home, and for just one pound, I could get a bowl of sweet peppers, or fresh button mushrooms or anything else that could fill that bowl. Over the years I was studying there, the market became one of my favourite places to shop and it was from there that I bought inexpensive trinkets to bring back for friends and family in Trinidad.

On one of my trips to the markets, I stumbled upon what looked like a mango, in a stall at the entrance. I could not believe my eyes. A big mango in England! Excitedly, I purchased the mango for less than a pound and quickly walked back to my room. I could not wait to peel the mango, and within minutes, with mango chow brimming to the top of my small bowl, I sat down to watch my favourite game show. Within an hour, both the show and mango were all gone! I must have returned to that mango stall countless times during my stay there, relishing this wondrous and delicious fruit, which I loved so much and which brought a taste of the Caribbean to me.

On one of my daily treks to the market, my eyes were drawn to a gothic-attired lady in the middle of the market, garbed in a long, black gown made entirely of velvet. I thought she was a vampire with the red lips, jet-black hair and long flowing cape. It did not help that she was next to a trinket stall selling strange, mysterious coloured stones and small bottles of potions. As I walked towards her, she offered one of the stones and the mysterious charms it held. Totally captivated by her spell, I enquired as to what did she actually do, and was disappointed when she said that she was a teacher in a secondary school and a writer showing me one of her published books! I am sure that this lady actually thought she was a witch and probably dabbled in the dark arts too! I never saw her again in the market but I have observed similar creatures walking the streets on occasion with no one batting an eye, and I concluded that this was quite normal in a not so normal town in the middle of England, where time seemed to have stood still. I too steered clear of these weirdly beautiful and mysterious people, not sure what to make them out to be.

But one of my favourite places was a small Chinese restaurant tucked away in a corner of the town, opposite the butcher's. It is there I was able to sit comfortably and eat a hearty meal of noodles in a broth with my choice of meats.

One Sunday, feeling a bit homesick, I was able to get curry rice and chicken which I ate with relish. So fond was I of this place, that it was one of the first places I visited to have a hearty meal after depositing my suitcases in my room. I am not sure if the people recognised me when I went there and I never spoke to anyone. But I found the Asian owners and waitresses warm and pleasant. I sensed a strong bond among the workers and the patrons who were mostly Chinese. If they were curious about me, they never showed it and I felt comfortable and happy eating alone while silently looking at the other patrons in the restaurant.

Years later, I would look back fondly at my early experiences in Coventry. I never forgot my surly cab driver, the shrill sound of the alarm which had me scampering out of the dorm barely dressed, the biting cold and the cupping experience in the little dark room or the gothic dressed lady in the market selling her strange potions. As I settled down to my life there, these experiences seemed less strange and over the years I drew comfort from the familiarity of the landscape and the places there.

The Antiquated Hotel at the Bottom of the Street

During my trips to Coventry, I developed a routine, which started with my nine-hour tiring flight from Trinidad, which left late in the afternoon and arrived early the following morning in Gatwick Airport. On arrival, I would purchase a bus ticket for the three-and-a-half-hour ride on the Express Bus to Coventry Pool Meadow station, which was located a five-minute walk away from the university and within very close proximity to the main hotel in Coventry.

The ride from the airport was effortless and the gentle roll of the large Express bus soon put most of the tired passengers to sleep. It was not unusual to see passengers, most of whom were students, wrapped in blankets, dead to the world. On my first trip, I was too nervous to fall asleep, afraid that I would miss my stop. It took every effort to keep my tired eyes open and to pay attention to the rolling landscape outside.

Unfamiliar with the landmarks, I alighted the bus at Warwick Station. Standing there, shivering in the cold, I must have cut a very pathetic figure. After a couple of minutes, I nervously asked the driver if this was Coventry station. Without expression, he indicated it was the next stop. Shamefully, I ascended the bus again and sat back down on my seat, hoping no one had seen me. Within an hour, I was deposited at Pool Meadow Bus Station with my suitcases.

Luckily for me, the university was in the centre of the city and it was easy to get a taxi to my contact in the International Office, only to discover that my accommodation was not ready. Hastily, arrangements were made for me to stay at a relatively inexpensive hotel, some distance away from the university.

But this early experience of the long trip from Trinidad to London and via the bus ride to Coventry, made me realise that I needed to have a convenient place of abode where I could recover the much needed sleep which I had lost on the journey and to reset my body clock by the four and five hours, England time.

In the following years, I decided to stay overnight at the old hotel across the street, it was within five minutes-walk from the bus station. The hotel was always gracious enough to give me an early check in after which I would stumble into my room, take a warm shower, drop the blinds and go to sleep for nine hours. This was my standard routine for the following years, prior to taking up my official residence in student housing. By the time I awoke, it would be late in the night and I would be famished.

On my first night there, the restaurant at the end of the ground floor corridor had already closed and seeing the adjacent bar still open, I ventured in and enquired whether I could be served some food. I was overjoyed when within a couple of minutes, a plate with a huge hamburger with fries was placed in front of me. Greedily, I ate every bit of food, sitting back to relax in the warm interior.

I soon discovered that this very antiquated hotel next to the University, had its own peculiarities. It was huge and its floors extended all the way across the street below. On one occasion, I actually lived a couple of weeks, in one of the rooms directly above the street! The rooms were reasonably large, with discoloured lace curtains hung sloppily on the glass windowpane. The floor was covered with a dusty brown carpet which looked like it was placed there when the hotel was built.

The bathroom was especially cold and unfriendly; bare fit of a bathmat, it left me muttering loud expletives every morning when I went to shower. The bathtub, which served as a shower was huge and I had to hold on to the side bars for dear life to get into the white, Victorian tub fearing that I would topple into the huge bath and hurt myself.

Next to the sink was a silver heater rack which I used conveniently, to dry all of my hand-washed clothing, saving a few pounds in the process.

The room also had an outdated television set which showed only three channels: BBC 1, BBC 2 and Sky TV and during the nights, I would snuggle deep under the covers, watching mostly game shows and documentaries. Occasionally, I would be lucky to see a good drama but even these seemed to be old reruns. During these years, I also rekindled my love for reading and would spend considerable time reading historical novels especially on Coventry.

But the hotel had a few redeeming qualities, the room was huge and provided a tray with cups and saucers, an assortment of English tea and coffee together with small packets of biscuits, which I loved to eat late in the night, before going to bed, and first thing when I got up in the morning. Over the time I was there, I would purchase breads, cereals, milk and other light foodstuff to eat in the room, placing the milk to chill on the cold window still.

It also had excellent cleaners who would leave my room spick and span every day. It was always a delight to return to the hotel after a long day to find the rooms cleaned by persons whom I rarely saw.

On one of my visits, I was upgraded to a new suite and was stunned when I opened the door to realise that it was a newly decorated honeymoon suite, in all red! In amazement, I looked at the queen sized, four-poster wooden bed with its red covers and equally red love seat leaning against the red walls. The room also had an old armoured set where I imagined the bride would sit and take off her make-up and prepare for the night. It was not my idea of a honeymoon suite rather more like a sleazy room in a downtown brothel.

As I hesitatingly walked into the room, I glimpsed a door to the side of the room leading unto a small balcony. I quickly opened the door and stepped outside, breathing in the cool air and readjusting my eyes to the scenery outside. Although I stayed there for the short period, I was in Coventry, I was very uncomfortable in that room. The wall must have been very thin because one night I was kept awake by a group of noisy, drunk women who must have spent the weekend attending one of the city's festivals.

I was told that they had just refurbished the room and was testing it out! I was alone, so I was not sure why they put me there. They never did get my views on that very red room and over the years, thankfully I was not placed there again.

One Sunday morning, I was awakened to loud singing, coming from either above me or somewhere down the corridor. For a moment I thought I was dreaming as I opened my eyes and peeped over the covers. Gingerly, I got off the small bed and tiptoed cautiously across the room, and placed my right ear to the door. Disbelievingly, I realised that I was, in fact, hearing gospel singing coming from the floor either above or below me. On enquiring at the lobby later in the morning, I was told that church services were held there by a particular religious group, each Sunday! Highly unusual, given that the cathedral was literally adjacent to the hotel.

If I thought that was odd, I was fascinated by some of the persons who patronised the hotel regularly. On several occasions, I saw a few bent, old biddies with white hair, stream in to eat the sumptuous and relatively inexpensive meals which were served daily in the restaurant on the ground floor. On the few occasions I ventured to eat there, I could not help but think how British it all looked, the Victorian styled room with its dark chairs and tables populated with these white-haired ladies and gentlemen, delicately picking at their plates while being served by equally white waiters and waitresses.

This was in stark contrast to the hotel's guests who included people of different ethnicities, speaking languages that I did not recognise. I loved sitting in the lobby and looking at the colourful and elaborate clothing of some of the guests checking in and out of the hotel. Many of them seemed to come from different parts of Africa, China and India.

Over the years I studied there, I grew very fond of that hotel which I embraced as my second home. Ritualistically, I would spend my first night there prior to taking up university housing. I had no connection to the people who worked there, rarely recognising a familiar face on each visit. But there was a familiarity and cosiness to the place which I liked, even with its antiquated furnishings and décor.

Castles on a Cold Winter's Day

During my first semester, one morning I awoke to find the room colder than usual. Gingerly, I stepped out of bed and walked over to the small window in the corner of my room. I opened the window and peered outside feeling the cold draft hit my cheeks. As I stretched out my arms, I felt the sharp coldness of ice and on closer examination realised they were white flurries melting in my hands. It was my first experience of snow in England. I quickly put on my coat and scampered outside, excited to walk on a white, fluffy mat of snow for the first time. It was reported that it was the first time in about twelve years that it had snowed in the UK.

Although my room was bitingly cold, outside was surprisingly warmer than I thought. I do not know whose idea it was to conserve energy by deliberately cutting the heat off for long periods during both the day and night. To keep warm, I would put on layers of clothing, including winter coat and socks with boots on, in my room. I would also sit directly with my back to the heater to warm up my cold body and paid dearly for it in the following days by developing severe back pain which would not go away.

But there are some places like Kenilworth Castle in which the snow adds a dreamlike aura enhancing the ethereal quality of the ancient ruins. I had journeyed there with two of my dear Trinidadian friends who lived in London and dutifully visited me during my internships at Coventry University. Their short visits were always something to look forward to, and we would spend time exploring the countryside during the day and in the night hovel in my small room with a bottle of wine or a cup of English tea and good conversation until the wee hours of the morning.

On that frosty morning, we took a bus by Pool Meadow station to make the brief trip to the castle. We did not notice the distance since we soon became engrossed in a healthy and passionate argument on politics, at the rear end of the bus. I was conscious that the bus had become very quiet as all ears were tuned in to this lively debate. At one time, I noticed the bus driver looking curiously at us in his rear-view mirror, perhaps accustomed to stony silence from his passengers. Suddenly, the bus came to an abrupt halt and the driver pointed to the castle some distance away, indicating that we should get off there.

Hesitantly, we stepped out of the bus, and asked if we were in the right place since I could see no road to the castle. "Yes, that way," he said, pointing to a track behind an old garage, driving off and leaving us standing there on the side of the street.

Not for the first time, I wondered about the foolhardiness of English drivers, who had the knack of dropping off passengers everywhere except at the entrances of buildings.

Left with little choice, we pulled our coats closer to ward off the draughty air and walked determinedly in the direction of the castle, through a damp, beaten down grass track, next to a small pond with swarms of small ducklings swimming lazily around, until we reached a road, on the other side of the meadow. I swear, I had seen this scene in one of my primary school books.

My adventurous friends, not to be deterred, walked on the narrow track to the side of the castle walls, muddied by the recent rains and chilled air, until we arrived at the entrance of the splendid Kenilworth Castle.

Suddenly, the castle seemed to hover menacingly over us as we walked up the street, arriving at the back entrance which was closed to the public. As I looked at the ruins of this impressive castle on that cold, wintery day, I thought I had just stepped into a different world. It reminded me of the castle described by William Shakespeare in his book *Macbeth*. This may not be too far- fetched since it was well-known that this famous playwright was born in the neighbouring village of Stratford-on-Avon in Warwickshire, not far from Kenilworth Castle, and he was rumoured to draw inspiration from the medieval towns and buildings there. It was also documented that Shakespeare performed a number of plays in the open-air theatres, in Coventry, during his early life there.

As I looked around at the huge grounds spread out for as far as the eyes could see, I imagined that in those ancient times, how usual it would have been to see gallant warriors astride their strong steads, galloping back and forth to the castle or the lone carriage carrying the elegant and graceful lady of the castle. Looking around at the ruins of what must have been one of the grandest castles in England, I imagined how different it would have been in those times and how sad to see what has now become of it.

The castle built by Lord Dudley, the married lover of Queen Elizabeth to impress his beloved, was truly a romanticist dream come true. The gardens were large and beautifully manicured with rows of what would probably have been English flowers including many varieties of roses, as far as the eyes could see. From where we stood, I could see hundreds of mossy steps leading up to the main entrance of the castle perched majestically atop the steep stairs. I imagined that many of the modern-day renditions of the famed story of Cinderella must have drawn inspiration from this magnificent and spectacular entrance.

As we entered the castle, or what remained of it, my eyes surveyed the shells of empty rooms, now left open to the elements because of its state of decay, trying to discern the secrets that they once held. As I reached the far end of the castle, I looked up to see a rickety, wooden stair leading to the skeletal remains of what looked like the upper floors of the castle, now completely destroyed except for the glassless window panes.

Gingerly, we made our way up the stairs, from where we got a bird's eye view of the castle remains and the spread of the extensive surrounding grounds. I marvelled at the grandeur of this place, still discernible in its tall widows, now without its glassed protection and its forgone glory, it was a reminder of a different world in a different place and time. As I surveyed the soft mat of green grass which covered the open dirt floor, I felt saddened to see such a wonderful place go to such waste.

As I surveyed the empty rooms from where I stood, I wondered if these lovers ever thought that one day this embattled castle which was built out of passion and defended with lives, will be left to ruins and become a shadow of its former glory, its ghosts only awoken by curious gazes and probing eyes of strangers from distant places. The walls of the castle may have protected them from the elements, conquest and seizure but it could not protect them from the passage of time and its foregone conclusion. I am sure that we too would become like these ghostly figures someday, remembered only by empty buildings and tales told over time.

As I wandered around this dilapidated castle, I wondered about the passion of the married lover of that regal lady, Queen Elizabeth and how deeply Lord Dudley must have felt to build this splendid castle to impress the one he loved, with the hope that she would be enticed to remain there with him. How much tears, pain and anguish of unrequited love did this castle hide in its walls? How many passionate and secret encounters did its hidden chambers conceal from the curious eyes? I felt oddly pleased that the story of their love seemed to have transcended time and lived on through these fables, to be told to all who visited. Although, in my travels around the world, I have visited many castles, I never forgot my visit to Kenilworth Castle on that cold, wintery day.

On the following day, we visited the nearby Warwick Castle and although it was done on a wintery afternoon, it did not evoke the same feelings. I was astounded by the grandeur of the grounds, the spectacular drawbridge at the entrance and the perfectly preserved, magnificent castle with its high turrets emanating from the main corners of its high-walled fortress, protectively spanning the entire circumference of the castle. During one of my visits, I adventurously decided to climb the winding stairs of one of the turrets. I immediately regretted this decision. The cold, dark, narrow passageway which led steeply upwards made me claustrophobic and scared. I felt like I had entered hell and there was no turning back. By the time, I had reached the top, I was less impressed when I realised how high above the ground I was and all I could think about was how I was going to get back down those stairs. That experience must have evoked some unexplainable feelings in me because that very night I dreamt that I was being chased by a red-haired witch up the stairs.

The castle was built by William the Conqueror in 1068 and is situated in the bend of the River Avon.

In the medieval period, the sixteenth Earl of Warwick, Richard Neville was known to be a very powerful man in

English history and politics and was referred to as the 'Kingmaker', having been extremely influential in choosing at least two kings for the English throne.

As I walked through the great hall, I was astounded by its grandeur and splendour, the decorated silver, armoured horses; the walls of shiny spears and other artillery displayed for all to see; the hand sculptured, mahogany wooden chests left for the admiring gazes of its many visitors; and the walls of original portraits of past royalty, Dukes and Duchesses smiling down at us. As I got closer to the paintings, I marvelled at the precision of the painters' eyes and hands. I could discern little difference between the modern day still photos taken with a camera to these life-like depictions of those posing for these paintings.

Walking through the many bedrooms, I stood in awe of its lifelike sculptures and statues, theatrically displayed by the famous Madame Tussauds, to recreate scenes and people who once lived there. These caricatures seemed so real that when no one was looking, I stuck my hand out to touch one of the statues, to reassure myself that it was not a real person.

But the most impactful scene for me was the recreation of life in the basement where all the work took place such as the blacksmith prepping the horses for battle; the cooks preparing the sumptuous meals; the washer women and cleaners doing their daily chores while children played in the background. This realistic depiction of the backend of the castle demonstrated what life was like for the many hands that came together to ensure that everything ran smoothly in the castle. It seemed like everyone had a defined role to play.

As I walked to the back of the castle, I gasped at the self-sufficiency of the Duke of Warwick, with his own water mill which processed water from the river behind the castle. As I headed to the narrow lane leading out the castle towards the garden, I felt like Alice in Wonderland as my eyes beheld the many flowering plants, roses of all varieties, the burst of colours, the soft mat of grass and the wooden chairs draped lazily next to a small pond with water lilies, and green ferns and plants hanging from large mossy stones.

These two castles reminded me of a time in history when life was so different, when powerful men lived in patriarchal societies, managing the affairs of their castles with little interference from outside their walls, taking the law into their own hands when they needed to. It showed the disparity between the wealth and extravagance of the elite class and the utilitarian roles of their subjects. It was also a period when women had clearly subscribed roles in the household and in society. But it also showed that men ruled by passion – passion for their lands and in the case of Lord Dudley for their women, willing to do anything for the people and things they love. I wondered how far we have drifted from these ideals in the world today.

Strange Encounters

During my time in Coventry, it was not uncommon for me to engage strangers in conversation, on occasion, when I felt the need for company. Since, my time there was too short to make any lasting friends, I would generally eat alone in the school cafeteria, observing the faces of students studying there while trying to guess where they came from. Those who came from the same country would generally form a small group, going everywhere together. I guessed that they also lived together, making their time there an enjoyable one. Those who were there by themselves would generally walk about alone, staring ahead without eye contact, looking sad and lonely.

One day, as I was entering the third floor of my dormitory, my nose picked up a very familiar scent. As I followed the scent, down the corridor, I found myself literally outside my bedroom. Confused, I put my nose close to my door wondering if someone had entered my room by mistake. Not detecting anything there, I continued sniffing until I faced a door opposite my room which I never noticed before. As I inhaled, I got the full waft of 'saltfish'. It has to be my imagination or I must be hallucinating, I thought. How on earth could this smell be here, in this remote place in England – a smell which only Caribbean people are only too familiar with! I lifted my hand to knock on the door but pulled it back for fear that my imagination was getting the better of me. After all, what would I ask the person on the other side? Over the coming days, I kept a watchful eye on the room next door, hoping to spot the mysterious cooker of saltfish.

I was not disappointed. One day as I exited my room, I saw the silhouette of a tall, bereted young man striding down the corridor clothed in the Jamaican colours of red, black and green. As we approached each other, we both looked surprised, halting at the same time. We soon discovered that we were both from the Caribbean, I from Trinidad and he from Jamaica, and were living literally opposite each other for weeks without ever running into each other.

It did bring me some kind of comfort to know that my Jamaican colleague was my neighbour, though we hardly saw each other after. One day, I invited him over to share a meal of stewed chicken and rice which he ate with much enjoyment and relish. As we sat there talking and getting to know each other, it occurred to me how intimate the room was with the table next to the bed and the small kitchenette. I never invited him over again because it dawned on me that the smallness of the bedroom might send the wrong message to this young man who might be a bit lonely in this remote place. Although we shared contact details, we never saw each other again and I imagined that he had returned safely to his homeland long before I left. But during that semester, I was comforted knowing that a fellow West Indian was living next door to me.

One day, while looking for an empty chair in the cafeteria, I saw a lone young man occupying an entire table. I walked up to him and with his consent sat down to eat my meal. He told me that he was from Pakistan and that he had left his wife behind and being away from his family made him very lonely. We chatted a bit and then he casually asked me if I would go out with him. Embarrassed by his question, I declined his offer and hastily retreated from the table. I wondered how many vulnerable young ladies have been entrapped by these lonely, young men living away from their families, for long periods.

On another occasion, I was sitting at a formal function for international students. I found myself opposite a very attractive young man with piercing green eyes. I soon found out that he was from Turkey. I found the young man's stare a bit disconcerting. Perhaps, it was the colour of his eyes which seemed almost snakelike and mesmerising. After the function, it had gotten very dark, and as I walked out the building with my coat pulled close to my neck, I spotted two young Indian men walking in the same direction. I hailed them out, and asked if I could walk with them. They were two of the most polite young men I have ever encountered who graciously and protectively walked me to the dorm in the city centre, ensuring that I was in the building before departing. Both men were from India and whenever I met them, they were extremely deferential towards me, standing up whenever I entered the room. These young men must have come from humble backgrounds and I got the impression that they lived frugally trying to make ends meet.

In contrast, I soon noticed that the more affluent young Indian men rarely mixed with these two students whom I had befriended. One day, while chatting with this group, I noticed a very dark young man of Indian descent enter the cafeteria walking past his fellow countrymen without any sign of acknowledgement and recognition. The group I was talking too also ignored him. I enquired why there was no communication between them and this individual and was surprised to learn that he was from a lower caste. I did notice that they were lighter skinned and it occurred to me how real this caste system was for people of India. It dawned on me how remote India and its customs had become to me and those of my fellow East Indians born in the Caribbean.

I was also fortunate to meet a young woman from Ghana who became my dear friend. Studying for her masters, I was deliberately paired with her by my supervisor in one of our classes. She was very bright and hard-working. From her, I got a glimpse of the struggle of persons like herself who came there to study in the UK. She studied long hours in the library and worked part time to make up the money she needed to pay her bills. She was very dignified and kind-hearted and although I was much older than she was, we developed an easy camaraderie and friendship. During one of our classes, I was recounting the horrendous experience of 1990 coup when Trinidad and Tobago democratically elected government was overthrown by the radical Muslim group, the Jamaat-al-Muslimeen. She looked at me in amazement and said, "Coup, we in Ghana have 'coups'," indicating that this was a common occurrence in the politics of Ghana. I learnt from her some of the customs of her country and the traditional roles ascribed to females there. Over the years I spent there, we developed a warm friendship which we continued to maintain to this day.

My class of eclectic students also included two young men from Pakistan. Although they were both around my age, they appeared much older. From their discussions in the classroom, I was able to gain a better understanding of the difficulties of living in a country riddled by constant conflict and battles. One of them spoke about the personal jails which the wealthy, and I suspect, politically corrupt people built in that country and how easy it was for civilians to take the law into their own hands. People seemed to disappear without questions being asked as if this was a norm in that part of the world. One of them spoke about the persecution of his family, his wife and parents and I suspect that he had fled that country for asylum under the guise of seeking higher education in the United Kingdom. Victimisation, political persecution and death seemed to be part of his reality and I wondered about his mental state of mind. I thought how lucky I was to live in a free society such as Trinidad and Tobago. These experiences as told by my colleagues gave me a deeper appreciation of my life here in the Caribbean.

On another occasion, I met a very curious middle-aged woman in the dorm's lobby. The housekeeper, perhaps trying to ensure that we were both not lonely, introduced us. She was very articulate and knowledgeable and talked incessantly about 'big' things. She appeared to have worked in the Justice system in one of the Indian states and wanted to meet the vice chancellor to discuss an important mission while there. She had a sense of importance and purpose, and coming from a university background with my own experiences and having worked in politics, decided to say little. She indicated that she was here alone and that given her customs she did not go out neither did she know anyone here. Knowing that her room was a couple of doors down the corridor, one Sunday decided to knock on her door and invite her out for an afternoon tea or coffee. As I approached the door, I head a heavy male voice, deep in conversation behind the doors. As I knocked, the room went completely silent. After a couple of attempts, I walked away thinking nothing of it. I decided to try again a couple of days later, same sounds and same non response. I decided I was not going to ask again. But one day, while returning from the university, she was speaking to someone and as I passed by, she paused to ask if I would wait and walk back to the room with her. I politely declined indicating I had another engagement, which was true. I remembered the curiously condescending look she gave me, perhaps thinking I was deliberatively avoiding her. I never saw her again, and I do believe that she had found alternate accommodation elsewhere.

I later learnt that Coventry was a world peace centre and that people from all over the world, for all kinds of reasons, found a safe sanctuary there. As I walked the streets alone, I wondered what deep, dark secrets these strangers held in their bosom. I never asked again and kept my own counsel, and not for the first time, I realised how fortunate we were in the Caribbean.

Crazy Bus Ride to Avon

I was sipping a cup of coffee in the town-centre one day, when I glimpsed my Nigerian friend passing by. I hastily made my way out to meet her. As we chatted excitedly in the street, I invited her to have coffee with me. She had completed her programme in the University and was about to submit her final work. She lovingly touched the blue binder of her completed thesis which contained her ticket to her master's degree. Having gone through this process, I understood her exhilaration at having a copy of her bound research, representing the culmination of a year of hard work, ready for examination. As we chatted, we realised how much we had in common, especially reading. I enquired if she had visited Shakespeare's birthplace in Stratford-on-Avon. Nodding in the affirmative, she indicated that it was easy to get a bus from Fairfax Street for a minimal fee to go there. I had visited once before but that was a long time ago. Having nothing much to do that afternoon and feeling in an adventurous mood, I asked if she would be willing to go there with me now. Just as eager as I was to make the trip, we climbed unto the bus parked on the main street and set off for Stratford-on-Avon in neighbouring Warwickshire.

As we chatted, she indicated that her father was a pastor in Nigeria and that both she and her sister were studying in the United Kingdom. As she regaled me with the patriarchal customs of her country, I thought to myself, how similar this custom was to most male-dominated societies where women were generally expected to play a subservient role. And not for the first time, I thought how lucky we were in Trinidad where women had equal access to education at the tertiary level and where the girls were outnumbering the boys and outperforming them as well in their traditional areas of studies. I was even more pleased that we had a female prime minister to boast about at the time of writing.

I thought how enlightened her father was, a man of the cloth, to thumb his nose at these archaic traditions and ensure that both daughters had opportunities for a better life through education in the United Kingdom. I was very surprised how deferential she was towards me and kept referring to me as 'doctor' in her distinctive Nigerian accent. During the ride, her phone rang and I overheard her telling the person on the other end that she was on the bus with her friend who is a 'doctor'. I felt truly honoured to be held in such high esteem by my foreign friend, although I had not received my certification as yet.

As we journeyed into the countryside, I was able to appreciate the medieval towns of Warwick with its meandering and narrow streets and small houses perched almost on the pavement of the roads. From afar, I could see the top of the famous Warwick Castle, which I had visited some time ago with my family. I remembered walking up the walkway to the main entrance of the castle and thinking about the many horse drawn carriages with fully dressed ladies decked in their finery being transported to and from the castle.

As we neared the town, I was amazed at the serenity of the place. At the time we had visited, winter had not fully arrived, and there were still beautiful baskets of flowers of varied colours hanging from the light-posts, on the streets. As we walked towards Shakespeare's place, which had become a popular tourist destination, I observed the many shops with their goods for sale. One in particular attracted my friend, and we returned on our way back for her to purchase a large jar of sweets which she was going to distribute to the children at the church she attended in Coventry.

As we made our way to the visitor's site, a flood of people encompassed us. Shakespeare's home was a small cottage with essentials to meet the basic needs of people of his time – a small cot for a bed, candles, and a kitchen with basic utensils. People at that time needed so little, I thought. And for a man like Shakespeare, even less. I wondered how he felt sitting in this threadbare room, with a tapered light, writing those famous quatrains for his plays. Did he ever, in the remotest part of his mind think that he would become a legend for centuries to come? Was he driven by ambition or sheer creativity and talent? Why in that time, with all its problems, did he find solace in stringing words together and creating dramas in his head? I wish I knew some more about this legendary figure who had and continue to have a profound influence in Literature to this day. Even though I read for a degree in Literature and studied many of Shakespeare's plays, I still did not have a sense of who he was.

In Coventry, I discovered that he performed some of his plays to a street audience in a makeshift stage. He must have been a regular visitor to Coventry and walked those streets many times. Was he inspired by its charm and drawn into its quaintness as I do now?

As I exited the small cottage, I found myself in a very conservative and small garden to the back of the house, with rose vines clinging to the walls of the small cottage. I imagined that if he actually lived there, he must have sat in the small wooden bench, in the middle of the garden a thousand times as he conjured up his stories in his mind.

Very soon, the sun had sunk low and we slowly made our way back to the bus stop, to catch the last bus back to Coventry. When the bus arrived, we scampered up the stairs to sit above deck, to enjoy the drive back to the city. We had barely taken our seat when the bus hastily pulled off, almost toppling both of us to the floor. Laughingly, we quickly plopped back down on the seats, holding on for dear life to the rails in front of us, as the bus quickly sped off. We were busy chatting when I noticed a tree branch slammed into the side of the bus, scraping against the glass window pane.

Instinctively, I looked up only to find our bus racing through the narrow streets of Warwickshire, oblivious to the intersections and cars waiting to cross the streets. This enraged one driver in a small convertible who shouted at the bus driver to slow down, and when he failed to heed his warning, gesticulated to him angrily and calling him a 'wonker' at the same time. Although I had not heard the word before, I was sure it was akin to a cuss.

This did not deter the bus driver in anyway and he continued to drive at a very fast speed, whizzing past long, short, high, low and narrow streets, biting the edge of roads and almost knocking down pedestrians. Everything became a quick blur as the driver hastily made his way back to Coventry. I was relieved when the bus came to an abrupt halt outside Coventry museum. Hastily, we scrambled out of the bus, peaking at the bus-driver on the way out. We were both astounded to discover that the driver was a female. Meeting our inquisitive eyes, she muttered a half apology under her breath in a barely audible voice. However, I was able to pick up the slurred speech and I came to the conclusion that she had one too many pints of beer, prior to driving the bus.

Over the time I spent in Coventry, on more than one occasion, I witnessed this lack of restraint in drinking by some of its inhabitants. On late afternoons, I would pass by one particular pub and from a distance, I would hear the noisy banter of that overzealous crowd which spilled out into the pavement. One day, I ventured into the pub to get one of its sumptuous hamburgers and was startled to hear a loud thud in the floor above. Within seconds, I was staring into the bloodied face of a young man who drunkenly stumbled out the building. Without much ado and with my heart pounding frantically, I grabbed my handbag and exited the pub minus my food. I never was tempted enough by its food to venture into the pub again.

As I walked towards my dorm, I thought what a close call we had on our drive back to the city. Luckily for me, my sense of security and safety though shaken a bit, quickly returned and I continued to explore the historic towns and sites around Coventry. I kept in touch with my friend, following her academic pursuits and was elated when in time, she too was awarded her doctorate in her chosen field of study and to build a career in academia as I did.

The Family Visit

During my first year of residency, my husband and teenage daughter made the long journey across the Atlantic to visit me for the first time. It was their first trip to the United Kingdom and I forewarned that the weather was cold and that they should be attired in warm clothes. Knowing that they were unfamiliar with the place, I mapped out clear directions on how to get to the midlands from the airport using the National Express. The journey from Gatwick Airport on the bus was almost four hours long and given that the trip took nine hours to get to the UK, one generally was extremely exhausted by the time they entered the bus. On my first trip, I was pleasantly surprised to find the bus heated and the ride very smooth. The gentle roll of the bus was almost like rocking a baby to sleep and it did not take long for all the tired passengers to be fast asleep.

On the designated day of arrival, with my hands filled with warm jackets, I excitedly made my way down the street to meet them at the bus station. From a distance, I could see them standing outside the bus station, looking disoriented and cold. They looked so happy and relieved to see me, and I too was elated to see them, not believing that they were actually there in front of me. As we hugged with joy, I quickly made them put on their insulated jackets to keep warm. My daughter's lips were quivering and I could feel her cold, tiny, little hands in my own. I hugged her even tighter trying to warm her up. My husband, even though cold, put on a brave face and I saw his look of confusion as his eyes roamed the area around him, probably trying to get his bearing. From the bus station, Coventry could appear cold and uninviting to strangers, especially during the winter period. Grabbing one of the suitcases, we made the short trek to the dorm where I was staying.

They were tired, but I also knew that they would be hungry, so as soon as we dropped off the suitcases in my room, I took them to my favourite restaurant to get some Chinese food. They were too jet lagged, after the long flight and willingly allowed me to take charge of them. It took them a relatively short period to acclimatise and my husband who did not like to travel outside of our home country, was comfortable enough, over the coming days, to roam about alone in the town. He soon discovered the 'One Pound' shop and each day would return happily with tins of canned food such as oxtail soup and red beans which he recooked and made delicious meals for us, in my room. He also found the Butcher's shop and excitedly returned one day with a large pork leg to cook, in my small stove.

Over the coming days, I was excited to show them some of the places which I had grown to love in Coventry especially the ruins of St Michael's Cathedral, the Victorian styled houses, the market and shopping areas and the famed Godiva statue in the city square. I also took them to Coventry Transport Museum which was within walking distance from the Britannia Hotel, and the small historical museum located in the University close to the Herbert Art Gallery.

I was excited to take them to see the majestic Warwick Castle which had been converted into a major tourist attraction, hoping that this would excite my young daughter. Those few days were happy ones for us after being away from each other for so long.

During that time, I also invited my sister and her husband from the United States, to visit as well. They had chosen to spend a few days in London, prior to coming down to Coventry. On the designated day, we excitedly made the short trek to the train station, to meet them. After about an hour, and the passing of a number of trains without any sign of them, I began to fear that they somehow missed the train or the stop to Coventry. My thoughts were interrupted by my ringing phone only to be told by my sister that they were at the Pool Meadow Bus Station.

My sister had boarded the bus instead of the train, although I had given her clear directions and we agreed that this was her mode of transport and that I would meet her at the designated time. As I grabbed a taxi, and quickly headed to the bus station, I could not help but exclaim aloud about how she did not listen. She was too excited and happy to see me and to be there in Coventry to care! Like me, she was exhilarated by the adventure she had embarked upon. She laughingly dismissed my sisterly buff, indicating that it was better to take the bus since she got to see the country on the drive over. I thought it better not to pursue the topic and let her bask in her excitement.

That night, we headed to an Indian restaurant to have dinner to celebrate. The food, which comprised a number of curries were delicious. Coming from Trinidad, we only knew one type of curry, the powdered one which we had to fry first before eating it. But in the United Kingdom, with their large Indian population, both from India and Pakistan, there were much more varieties and colours to choose from. I particularly liked the red Thai curry sauce and discovered that they were sold in small glass jars in one of the main stores and made cooking curry so easy.

During dinner, my sister with her American accent, seemed to have impressed the male Indian waiter and he became demonstrably, overly friendly asking all sorts of questions about life and work opportunities in the United States. At one point, totally exasperated by his intrusiveness and her accommodating behaviour, I tried to shoo him away. But he refused to take the hint and arrogantly dismissed me as if I were the one intruding in his party. I must have given my sister a hard look because she seemed to have gotten the message and ended the conversation abruptly as we got back to our family dinner. I never went there afterwards, and the following year they must have closed shop since the sign had disappeared, together with the waiters. I wondered if he ever got to the United States and the opportunities he felt awaited him there.

We had planned to do so many things during their brief visit but got around to doing so few, waking late in the night, drinking wine and chatting incessantly about everything and nothing. My sister, Angela and I are very much alike and share similar interests which included politics. It did not take us long to become fully engaged in a robust political discussion about local politics in our home country. Even though she lived in New York, she continued to take a deep interest in our politics and used every opportunity to voice her opinions. Many times, our conversation became so passionate that few people ventured to get between our heated debates. I was extremely touched that she had journeyed all the way from New York to spend a few days with me in England.

Time went by quickly and before we knew it, it was time to catch the bus for London where we were going to spend a few days, before heading back to our respective home countries.

But that vacation was most memorable because of the easy camaraderie amongst all of us, the novelty of being in this quaint town and having my loved ones with me made it very special time in my life.

I still remember sleeping in that little bed and hugging the small frame of my young daughter so tight, not believing that she was actually there with me after not seeing her for months. I was so happy to see my husband comfortable enough to roam the town alone, enjoying the little things which made him happy.

Although in the years to come, we tried to organise another vacation together, it never really quite worked out. But this was truly a very special time for all of us.

The Grand Dame:
In Remembrance of
Pat Bishop

I had always felt safe in Coventry, but that security was shattered on my third year when I returned to the university for my short stay. I am not sure what exactly caused it; if it was because of a rather unusual experience I had while in Trinidad which may have disturbed my oftentimes calm composure. I was part of a committee of some of the most creative and renowned minds in the country. The Minister of Government himself having straddled both academia and politics, seemed inclined to marry both professions to create a very innovative fusion of minds and spirits to develop a policy for the creative sector in commemoration of the country's fiftieth anniversary celebrations. I do believe that he wanted to incorporate some academic thinking in the conceptualisation phase and to give us some experience by placing us young academics to work with these creative minds.

I was very honoured to be part of that committee and stood in awe of people like Peter Minshall, renowned for his spectacular and dramatic creations such as tan-tan and saga-boy, two gigantic, lifelike human floats on stilts, representing two legendary folklore Trinidadian figures. A man who was once co-opted by the Olympic Committee to create a spectacular opening ceremony for one of its Olympic Games. Sitting in that committee, I was able to get an insight into how these creative minds worked and was awed by their open honesty, passion and frank expressions.

I saw the insane passion which fuelled their creativity and their pain of being born into a landscape which did not understand, recognise and support that deep spirit and their outpourings represented in their art-forms. I empathised with their frustration of inadequate resources and unrealised dreams. I was so proud of these people whom I deeply admired for their talents and their ability to chase after those elusive dreams, in spite of the challenges they faced.

My country, still in its embryonic stage of creative development, did not see the potential of this very important sector as key to moving the country forward. After all, in a land where oil is king and education was seen as an end it all to a grander corporate life; few people especially those in power, really understood this group of people who were like a main ingredient to our very mosaic and cosmopolitan society.

They were not that receptive to the intrusion into their creative world by academia and I detected more than a hint of hostility towards the attempt to structure their thinking into a cohesive policy statement. On one occasion, during a presentation, an unknown name was called to do a presentation, and the grand dame of the committee, musical director Pat Bishop, looked down her bespectacled nose, mouthing the name of the person as if it were a foreign object that she could not wait to pulverise with her teeth and spit out. On another occasion, she barked at the over-exuberance of another young presenter as if she were a child playing grown up in her household – perhaps sensing the person's attempt at know-how when she really didn't know how! But she did take an unusual liking to me, perhaps sensing my own hesitancy and uncertainty within this eclectic group.

On one occasion, I got up to get a cup of tea and although my back was turned from the table, I felt eyes boring through me as if trying to understand who I was and why I was there. Midway to the coffee table, I stopped and turned around, looking directly into those probing eyes and timidly asked if she would like a cup of coffee, expecting her to pin me with her harsh gaze, as a butterfly being dissected on a table. In an instant, I saw conflicting thoughts flit briefly over that stern face, then those fierce eyes softened and she smiled nodding at me with approval and saying no at the same time. Perhaps, I had conveyed the respect that I felt that she deserved and indicated to her at the same time that she was someone whom I admired and was in awe of. I wanted to learn and I suppose as a teacher at the university, she was open to imparting knowledge. Whatever it was, I felt that we had connected in some fundamental way and that she had given me a pass to be on the committee, not as an equal but as a student.

During lunch break, she chose to sit next to me in the small, round table which I occupied in the eating area and in a contemplative mood, as if talking to herself, she stated sadly that she had done this so many times and she felt that nothing ever came of it. Referring to the many times she had sat on similar committees by different regimes. The eternal optimist, I tried to reassure her and calm her turbulent mind by saying that we must always have hope, if nothing else and perhaps this time, things will be different. She nodded her head in deep contemplation and after a few minutes leaned over and confidentially whispered, "Did I get on bad?" referring to her explosive reactions in the committee.

At a loss for words and deeply moved by her show of softness, I said, "No, you are who you are and you should say what you have to say." She was silent for the rest of the lunch period, retreating into her own thoughts, oblivious to the people and the conversation taking place around her.

But I always remember, one of her most memorable words which erupted from her during one of her frustrated outbursts, "What we do, we do because we have to. Nobody asks us to do it. We just do it!" indicating that the creative spirit was a force of its own which could not be contained or controlled and that it flowed from her body and soul, like a river without an end, pouring out creations, like shiny pebbles on a riverbank.

On that ill-fated meeting which was held on a Saturday morning in the Minister's office, I entered the room a bit late and saw this motley group sitting grumpily around the table. I gingerly made my way towards the vacant seat, next to the dear lady but just as I was about to sit down, I suddenly had a change of mind and moved to another seat, away from her, not wanting to start my morning on a sour note. Her eyes followed me silently and expressionlessly as I took my seat away from her and although she looked at me, I felt that she really did not see me, her mind far away in deep thoughts, in a world of her own. There was a melancholy air about her but I dismissed it thinking that perhaps she was not happy to be dragged from her house on a Saturday for a cause that she really did not believe in. We were deep in conversation around the table, some more vociferous than others, when a soft gasp was heard at the end of the table and we saw our grand dame slumped over the table unconscious. As panic set in, water was fetched in the hope of reviving her, but to no avail. In a frenzy, attempts were made to call an ambulance which arrived belatedly to take her to the hospital. As I moved away with a deep heart and sinking feeling, I was handed a pair of shoes belonging to her. I looked down at those plain, simple shoes and wondered at their smallness for such a grand lady. I walked heavily towards the side of the room and for some inexplicable reason, as they trolleyed her out of the room, I turned my back, not wanting to see her in this condition, perhaps fearing the worst. I could not explain it, but I knew she had already gone and even when the news came a couple of hours later, I had already known her sad fate.

I did not know her well but I felt her loss as if I had known her all my life. It touched me to the core and I mourned her passing as if she were one of my close relatives. And even though, I rarely attended funerals, I felt obliged to go to the Trinity Cathedral on that sombre day, to attend the memorial mass, in Port of Spain. As I sat alone in one of the pews of that ancient cathedral, I marvelled at its splendid architecture, and I recalled her poignant question of how many persons acknowledged these remarkable, historic buildings and took the time to experience the living art forms in our society, expressing her love for the buildings left behind, a reminder of our once glorious days as a colony and registering her disappointment of a still primal society in many respects.

It was a similar sentiment which I heard from literary icon and Nobel Laureate Sir Vidya Naipaul, during one of his visits to Trinidad. Both Pat Bishop and Vidya Naipaul spent considerable time in England, Naipaul living there for most of his life. Both had seen the long lengths the British went to, to preserve all aspects of their history, salvaging everything so that future generations would not forget where they come from and the richness of their past as they shape their present. They could not understand that for all our talk of development that we were so underdeveloped in many ways and would indiscriminately tear down these treasures replacing them with modern, commercial, concrete buildings covered with glass.

By the time I arrived at Coventry, the memory of that traumatically sad experience was still fresh in my mind. On my first night there, I awoke in the middle of the night, sweating profusely. She had come to me in a dream. I dreamt that I was riding a bus outside Coventry City and I was visiting a historic town with its archaic buildings probably dating back to the fifteenth century. Suddenly, she appeared from nowhere and in amazement, I went to kiss her on the cheek, as one would do with a dear friend, but alas, the lady turned away her face not wanting me to kiss her. Perhaps, the starkness of that dream and the rejection of the kiss woke me in a startled and confused state, unable to distinguish dream from reality. After all, it was so real! In the morning, I walked dazedly around Coventry's centre and in my sleep deprived state must have unconsciously bumped into a mysterious, cloaked stranger, in that cold, frosty morning. As I looked up, I saw the normally indifferent face worn by most English people, turn to more than curiosity, perhaps misreading my intentions. I quickly moved away, but soon after turned around to see him walking just behind me. Perhaps, he sensed my panic and like a vulture decided to follow its prey, before swooping down on it. I suddenly felt scared for the first time, realising that I was alone in this remote place in England. Suddenly, this magical place seemed cold and unfriendly and I felt vulnerable. I hastily walked back to my room which was located in the centre of the town not too far away from where I was walking, glancing backwards to see if he had followed me. It was with deep relief that I entered the building and my room, shutting the doors tightly behind me.

But this uneasiness continued to haunt me over the coming weeks and my otherwise safe sense of security which I normally felt, slowly began to dissipate. Now shadows seemed to lurk in the places which I normally visited, on my daily treks to the university. I noticed the unkempt, drunken young men lazing by the cobbled lane passing through the cemetery, outside the cathedral. The lonely streets seemed threatening and I no longer felt safe to be outdoors late in the evening as I was accustomed to doing and making the short trips to the ruined remains of the St Michael's Cathedral to sit quietly in one of its vacant chairs to watch the sun set. My experience with death in Trinidad had awakened my consciousness to the dangers of my surroundings and smashed my innocent view of this quaint town, destroying the magical and mystical feelings I had, revealing the underbelly of the seedier and more dangerous side of the city.

That serenity was dislocated further when early one morning, I awakened to see a young man on the roof of a building, not too far away from my bedroom window. I suddenly became aware that it was the summer period and most students were away from school and the dormitory where I was staying was virtually empty. My troubled mind wondered, if a stranger could slip through the doorway to the building or through the window to harm me. For that entire period, the dreamlike quality of the town was lost to me, and I for the first time, wanted to flee that place and return to the sanctuary of my home and family. Fortunately for me, the feelings were not permanent because by the time I had returned for another round of short stays there, that magical bubble had returned and I roamed the street as I did before, enchanted by its mystical quality, oblivious to any dangers around me.

But, I have reflected on my experiences on that committee. Since then several of its prominent members have died such as musical arranger, Jit Samaroo, that very quiet, little East Indian man who had some of the most fiercest steel pan players eating out of his hands because of his talent to arrange our music on the pan, played during our annual carnival celebrations, winning many titles during the steel pan festivals. He said little and did not have to, having earned his place among his peers as one of the greats of our society. Humble and sincere, he sat quietly and contemplatively on that committee, listening but not sharing his feelings or that mindscape it occupied. Pat Bishop, who conveyed so much meaning in a single sentence, that to this day, I think about what she had said about the creative spirit which lived inside of her and like a mother had to go through the gestation of pregnancy, the agony of labour until the birth of that creation. I could never forget that cultural icon and theatrical genius, Peter Minshall and the way he commandeered the committee in dramatic style as though he were an actor on stage, as he transported us with his ideas and language. I marvelled that the architect of that meeting, a creative spirit himself, recognised the potential of the human imagination and trying to harness these creative spirits to produce something truly great, during an important time in our country's history. For whatever reasons, I am happy that our paths have crossed and in this lifetime I had the opportunity to meet, interact and learn from these truly fantastical forces which came from the bosom of our country. They were the special ingredient which added that flavour which made our country so unique. I wondered if long after they have gone, if we would truly understand and appreciate the contribution of these cultural legends in defining our society.

My Encounter with Nobel Laureate Sir Vidya Naipaul

During the time I spent alone in Coventry, I could not help but reflect on some of the early Caribbean authors who had made this journey to England, for similar reasons. As a colony of Great Britain, colonials had the privilege of living and working in England, as a result, a number of Trinidadians journeyed there in search of a better life. I vividly recall the writing of Samuel Selvon's *The Lonely Londoners* when I was studying Caribbean Literature in school. The description of London was that of a cold, bleak place where life was hard for those who made the journey there from the colonies.

However, author V.S. Naipaul had the most profound effect on me as a young student through his writings of *Mimic Men* and *Miguel Street*. These books had distinctly different styles of writing and showed different sides to this controversial author. In *Mimic Men*, the long prose written about people in Trinidad left me slightly disturbed about the type of society in which we lived. At that young, impressionable age, it was difficult for me to understand the darkness in his writing and his need for inflicting pain unto himself. The world which he painted seemed so lonely and unhappy and I felt that he was a lost soul in the universe. However, when I read *Miguel Street*, I laughed so hard, my head started to hurt, and tears rolled down my eyes in sheer pleasure. The stories were so real, and coming from a small village in the country, I could have identified with each of the characters in his book.

I was fortunate to have met this legendary writer at The University of the West Indies where I worked. In April 2007, he was invited to be part of the Nobel Laureate series conceptualised by campus principal, Dr Bhoendradatt Tewarie who was a disciple of Naipaul having studied his works in University and gained his doctorate in Comparative Literature with a focus on Naipaul writings. Therefore, bringing Naipaul to Trinidad was akin to bringing royalty to visit the university. Much thought went into planning and preparation for his visit and I was given the task of finding the right place for him to stay during his short visit. I soon discovered a beautiful mansion owned by an aged and ailing foreigner, who had come here to retire and live out the rest of his life. By the time we had leased the property with housekeeper et al, the goodly gentleman had passed away and the property was left to his housekeeper. The mansion was less than ten minutes from the university and was properly secured to give the Naipaul contingent a sense of safety within its luxurious walls. When they arrived there, they seemed very happy with the elaborate accommodations.

The first time I met Sir Vidya was at an official meeting in the Principal's Office and I could not help but think that for a frail looking man how sharp his mind was. He probably first saw me when I handed him the guest book to sign, not showing any sign of acknowledgement as he lovingly turned the yellowed pages of the large, historic document, looking admiringly at some of the famous names inscribed in the book.

Naipaul had very small eyes, almost like two slits across his face making it hard to read his expression. His bearded face appeared soft, belying the rumours of his harshness as carried in the international press. When I saw him get up with much difficulty, I felt an immediate sense of warmth and tenderness towards him as one would with an elderly relative. I instinctively wanted to go and assist him but retreated behind the large contingent of university officials. Naipaul was accompanied to Trinidad by his wife, his stepdaughter as well as his agent. The wife was a Pakistani national who rarely smiled and who hovered over him protectively and he too seemed highly dependent on her, forever looking around for her reassuring presence. His stepdaughter was a very beautiful and gentle young woman whom Naipaul seemed very fond of, his eyes softening every time he looked at her. The agent, a tall, white-haired gentleman from England, said few words and silently accompanied the entourage wherever they went.

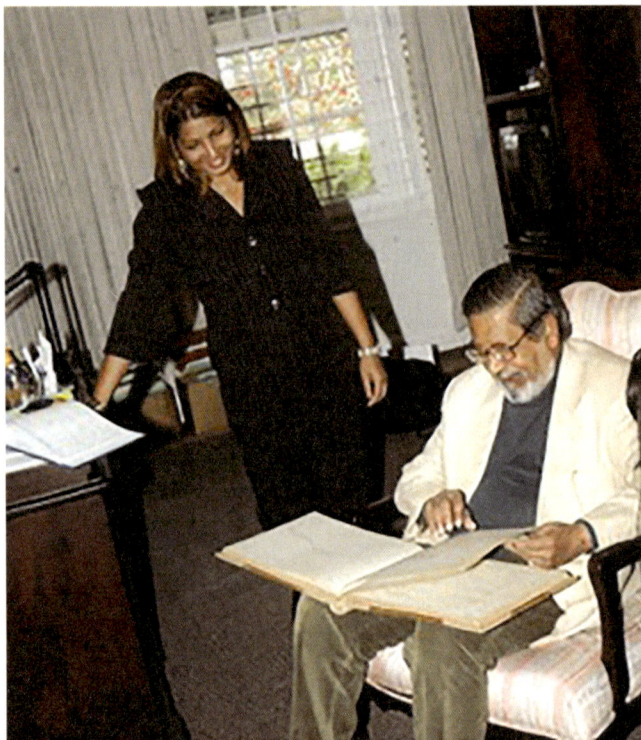

Sir Vidya admires the UWI guest book at the office of the campus principal, UWI St. Augustine Campus while I look on.

My duties included briefing Naipaul daily on his agenda so that he could be prepared for the day's activities. This packed agenda involved an elaborate book signing ceremony at the university's auditorium, public lectures and appearances at both the university and select high schools. Some of these did not go as expected and created some negative press in the media. The press conference to introduce

Naipaul to the local press did not get off on the right note. The press was in full attendance but it seemed that Naipaul was not pleased with some of the questions posed by the press and became a bit antsy. Lady Nadira seemed especially irritated, having spotted Nobel Laureate Derek Walcott's daughter in the audience. I was very relieved when the press conference came to an end and the contingent departed.

But there were other problems too which we did not anticipate. A conflict occurred between Lady Nadira and the housekeeper, and we were forced, at short notice, to move the entire contingent to the Hilton Hotel in Port of Spain. I transported Naipaul's agent and stepdaughter in my vehicle while Sir Vidya and Lady Nadira went in another. The drive to the hotel was tense and conversation stilted and I was happy to reach our destination. I recalled sitting next to Sir Vidya in the lobby while they prepared the room and trying to reassure him that everything will be taken care of. He said little, showed no emotion and mentally retreated from the room and the cacophony of noises around him.

However, during the time I was his liaison, I was fortunate to have some light moments with him and he actually seemed to like me. One morning, as I sat around the small breakfast table in the house he stayed, briefing him about the upcoming book signing, he leaned over to me in a friendly manner and asked my opinion as to what he should wear for the occasion. I indicated, in no uncertain terms, that he should wear something comfortable since people were interested in him as a personality and not his clothes. "But what colour should I wear," he insisted. I muttered something to myself, thinking that perhaps he did not hear me, only to get a response of "Yuh think ah deaf o what." Thinking I had heard wrong, I looked at him apprehensively only to see a large mischievous grin on his face. I do believe that he was having fun at my expense.

On the day for the book signing, as I busied myself ensuring that all the stage arrangements were in place, I noticed a rather terse contingent making their way on the stage. Thinking nothing of it, the group sat down for the discussion which was to precede the book signing ceremony.

Naipaul was at his best as he answered each question flawlessly, striking down those he did not think was his match, while matching wit with some of the most senior academics. The conversation was invigorating and exciting and one could not help but admire the immerse intellect and intelligence of this genius of a little man.

Very soon, the conversation ended to thundering applause by a very enthused and appreciative audience including the late ANR Robinson, former Prime Minister and President of Trinidad and Tobago. During the break, I was reliably informed that Naipaul who was a perfectionist was not all that pleased with the discussion on the stage, having felt that it had gone on too long and that some of the questions were too pedantic, taking out his spleen on the chair of the event. I was not sure why this particular academic seemed to irk him especially, but needless to say he was at a loss to retaliate. However, by the time he returned for the book signing, he was all composed and got down to the task of signing the hundreds of new books bought by Trinidadians for the ceremony.

Later in the night, the contingent was taken for an elaborate and leisurely dinner at a small, cosy restaurant in Port of Spain. I found myself sitting opposite Sir Vidya and during the conversation, he leaned over and casually asked me how it was to work for the campus principal. Without hesitating, I said that he was hardest on those who were closest to him and one learnt never to make an error twice with him. He seemed to like my answer and contemplatively slumped back in his chair to continue his dinner. I felt that although I spoke the words, he was able to read much more into what I said. I was touched that he was warm to me and seemed comfortable in my company to ask my honest opinion, perhaps realising that he would get an honest response from me.

Sir Vidya signs copies of his book prior to his departure at the Piarco International Airport in Trinidad.

On his last day on the campus, while awaiting his vehicle to take him back to his hotel, I took him into my office, a few steps down the corridor and he sat comfortably there for a couple of minutes, looking around and saying little. Having been a student of literature and an avid reader, I had a collection of his books, both old and new in my office. Spontaneously, I took them out and asked him to sign them. Without a flicker of emotion, he signed each copy and handed them back to me. I was very touched by his gesture since Lady Nadira had made it clear that he was only going to sign new books. One of the books was extremely old, I had gotten it in my in-laws' house, among a stack of old books and rescued it from being thrown away. He looked at the book with its yellow pages and worn out cover, signed it and handed it back to me. I gave the book to the Montrose Vedic School when my daughter graduated from her Secondary Entrance Exam. I hope that they treasure the copy and kept it for archival purposes. After all, a son of the soil, a born and bred Naipaul who lived in the 'Lion House' not too far away from the school signed the copy.

When Naipaul was ready to depart from Trinidad, I sat in the VIP lounge in the airport with his wife, stepdaughter and agent as they waited for the plane to arrive. I was taken by surprise when Lady Nadira turned to me and graciously extended an invitation to visit their home in London as Naipaul looked over approvingly. I graciously declined, not sure what to make of the invitation. But I felt sad to see him leave, having grown fond of him over the couple of weeks he was there. I felt too, that given his age and frail body, perhaps this may be his last visit to his homeland.

During my time in Coventry, I thought of my encounter with this legendary figure, who put little Trinidad and Tobago on the world map but who could not find happiness in his home country. His brutal honesty about the people of the Caribbean, especially his home country, made him very unpopular here and I felt that it was sad that for someone who had achieved international recognition and had such immense stature, that Trinidad and Tobago never truly appreciated or genuinely recognised his genius and talent. I feared that Naipaul did not revise his opinion about Trinidad and the type of society in which we lived. His visit was also met with some controversy in some quarters of society.

Up to the time of his death, he continued to be a controversial figure living out his life in his adopted home in London. I never forgot my encounter with him, the brief time I spent in his company, and will always treasure the memories which I have to this day.

Graduation

Exactly six months after completing my examination, a date was set for graduation at Coventry's magnificent ultra-modern, St Michael's cathedral, outside the main administration building, in the heart of the city. On my return to Coventry to receive my certificate, I was accompanied by my immediate family comprising my mother, husband, daughter, my elder sister and my niece. The trip took some planning on my part since I decided to make the best of the opportunity to show my family, especially my mother, parts of Europe, since this was her first visit there. My sister and her daughter were travelling from Montreal while we were departing from Trinidad. I booked us in a small hotel in London, within walking distance from the Euro station which would take us to Paris. For my sister, unaccustomed to travelling on trains, I had to map out her route from Heathrow airport to the small hotel in the city and hope for the best, since she was given to panicking very easily. I was very surprised when we arrived at the hotel that she was already there, sitting in a chair looking very relaxed, happy and excited at the same time, as if this was nothing out of the ordinary for her.

Sensing that this was a once in a lifetime opportunity for my family to travel together, I decided to extend the trip to include a visit to Paris also. This was done especially for my mother, who like me, had a deep interest in medieval churches and all things ancient. I wanted, especially, to show her the beautifully designed Notre Dame Church, located across the Thames River, with all its intricate designs and grandeur befitting of its ancient past. This trip had created such a deep impression on her mind that often times when we spoke in Trinidad, she would tell me how she could not believe that in her lifetime and in her wildest imagination that she would be able to visit this marvellous country and spectacular churches, which she only saw on television. Although, she visited other churches in Coventry during our visit, the Notre Dame created the deepest impression in her mind.

Instead of staying at my favourite hotel in Coventry right next to the university, I booked a hotel online and found one which purported to be less than ten minutes walking distance from the university. As we alighted the train from London late in the afternoon, we jumped into two taxis to take us to the hotel. As we were being taxied to the hotel, I realised that the journey was taking longer than anticipated through roads which I did not recognise. Curiously, I looked outside hoping to find a familiar landmark. My fears were temporarily allayed when the taxi stopped abruptly in front of a reasonably nice-looking hotel.

The hotel was relatively modern, unfortunately Coventry experienced a very hot summer and the rooms were inordinately hot leaving us uncomfortable in the nights. An appeal to the manager generated two small standing fans which were inadequate to cool the rooms. The manager was of Indian descent and became overly friendly towards us, and I suppose in hindsight he probably felt a sense of affinity since we appeared to be of the same ethnicity. This was furthest from the truth, since time and distance from our great grandparents' ancestral home in India and the mixing of ethnicities in Trinidad, had created its own fusion of cultures, which really was far removed from that practiced in India. I was uncomfortable around him and he must have sensed it because he did not engage me and for most of our stay there, we avoided each other.

My graduation ceremony turned out to be everything I had imagined. Bedecked in my long, blue robe with the trademark gold doctoral cape and hat, we made our way to the St Michael's cathedral for the graduation ceremony. I felt elated that I had made this journey and my hard work had finally paid off. I had overcome my own insecurities of not being able to finish in the designated three years, after being forewarned at my orientation ceremony, that this was highly improbable for a split-site student, studying remotely from the Caribbean. I had made up my mind there that I was going to do the impossible. It took courage to make the decision to leave my family home, especially my young daughter at a time when she needed me. It took sheer tenacity, to journey across continents, to this yet unknown university, to pursue my dream and it took dedication and focus to achieve this milestone in my life. But at the end, it was all worth it!

Graduation Day

As I sat with pride on the pew to the front of the church where the few doctoral students were placed, I admiringly looked at all the proud graduates and wondered what their journeys entailed and how many sacrifices they too had to make to reach so far. For me, I saw my entire study abroad experience flash before me, from the moment I came to Coventry for the first time, to my meeting with my supervisor, my first experience of snow, my moments of loneliness , the occasional visits and support of close friends and finally my viva where I had to defend my thesis.

I searched through the crowd for the more familiar faces of my family, sitting not too far behind. I was delighted to have most of them there to share my achievement – my husband and daughter who were very supportive during my studies abroad; my mother who stepped in to take care of my family especially my daughter, when I was away; and my sister for coming all the way from Quebec to be with me. It was with pride I heard my citation being read and the names of my two supervisors being called as I walked onto the stage to receive my award. I recalled how my supervisor and his wife celebrated me with dinner when I passed my examination and how elated by local supervisor was when I gave him the news over the phone – both of them overjoyed at my success. As I was handed my certificate, I felt obliged to break protocol and turn around and salute the platform party which included the Vice Chancellor, for having had this rare privilege and honour of studying and receiving this award from Coventry University.

Coventry will always hold a very special place in my heart and I would be eternally grateful to this institution for making my study abroad experience such a memorable and treasured one. I still cannot today truly give an explanation why I chose this relatively unknown university in the middle of England to pursue my doctoral studies. But I know now, as I knew then that it was the right place for me. I never regretted it for a moment and continue to consider this place a second home, returning from time to time to bask in its comforting and peaceful arms.

A few months later, at a special celebration at my house, I was overwhelmed to know that my accomplishment was seen as a family accomplishment and an inspiration to the younger ones pursuing their education. This was confirmed by the very moving speech by my younger brother who talked about 'our' challenges coming from a small village in a rural part of Trinidad. I was stunned to realise that my achievement was viewed as a village success, and I was so happy to see some of my childhood friends and cousins make the almost two-hour journey to celebrate this momentous occasion with me. I was happy to see my sister, my number one fan, journey from New York to share this time with me, although she could not be there at my graduation. Perhaps, one of the most moving moments was when my cousin Earl presented me with a glass plaque with my name etched on it! There is nothing so fulfilling as being celebrated by those near and dear to you. Though now deceased, I continue to look at the plaque in my living room as a remembrance of him and the tremendous pride he had in me. It was with pride that I listened to my daughter serenade me with song and my heart was filled to the brim to share this milestone event in my life with all my dear family, friends and loved ones.

The Pink Lady on the Train

As soon as we arrived in London from Paris en route to attend my graduation in St Michael's Cathedral, we boarded the first train to Coventry in the late afternoon. Unfortunately for us, I had bought the cheapest ticket, convinced by the ticket vendor that if we were in no hurry, we could save a few dollars by purchasing the proffered tickets. My time in Coventry had prepared me for the frugality of the English, known for their sensible nature and therefore not one to waste their hard-earned cash. I commend the English for their timeliness and orderliness, something we in the Caribbean did not see often. It took a while to get accustomed to their great sense of manners. My daughter could not help but notice this on her first trip to the UK, and excitedly told me how everyone was so kind and pleasant to her, saying 'thank you' all the time.

I bought the tickets and we headed to the first arriving train in Euston Station and was just in time to hastily jump on. English trains after all waited for no one. You either get on or get left behind. With at least six large suitcases in hand, this was a big challenge for our large family group to store them in the very small place designated at the end of the carriage. On a first come basis, this is very challenging as other passengers usually rush to get the space. I have seen people pushing and shoving their suitcases on the shelf above their heads for dear life, some hanging over passengers' heads, ready to fall at a simple jerk of the train. Boarding a train with a suitcase has become a nightmare for me ever since. My dear sister, seeing my dilemma, and not one to idly stand by, went into immediate action and quickly handed me the suitcases, one at a time as I stuffed them into the small space, hoping that they would all fit. My husband overwhelmed by the rapidity with which we moved simply got out of our way.

Alas, we realised that we were trying to achieve the impossible and at least three of the suitcases were left by the doorway behind the seats not too far away from where we stood. As we looked around for seats, we realised that all the seats were filled. How could this be? I have been travelling on trains in England and never had to stand, especially for such a long journey. I caught the sympathetic expressions of my fellow travellers, some of whom were hugging the back of the train, close to the bathroom, they too without seats. It was peak time and we had gotten on the slow train! Drat, how I wished I had spent the few extra dollars for another train with proper seating arrangements! As the train moved off, we held on for dear life all the time keeping an eye on our suitcases next to the doors, for fear that they would topple off the train when the door opened. Soon, we discovered that the train was going to make all the stops to drop off passengers who were leaving the city after work. This would double our time, I thought exasperatedly!

On about the third stop, a smartly dressed woman boarded the train. I could not help but admire her nice pink dress topped by high, pink, stiletto heels. As the train moved, she seemed to stumble and a fellow passenger, extended his hands sympathetically to steady her. I thought nothing of it, until I heard my big sister stifle a giggle. Looking in the direction of her gaze, I noticed our pink dressed lady was nodding off as she held on to the bars by the door. First her head bobbed left, jerked back to position, then bobbed to the right, then back again to position, while standing and holding on to the rail column next to her. This continued for some time and as I gazed at her intently, I realised that something was wrong. I concluded that perhaps she had a little too much to drink, perhaps with her colleagues in their after-work time. By this time, she had caught the eyes of the rest of our fellow passengers, standing at the back of the train, waiting for the inevitable to happen.

My mom, who had gotten a seat close to us, kept a watchful eye on the suitcase. Soon, she was signalling to me that the pink lady was aiming to sit on my suitcase which could not hold her voluptuous weight, since it was lightly packed. I could almost see the poor thing falling on her behind on the floor and rolling down the corridor of the train. I hastily made my way to her, arresting her posturing derriere from sitting down on the suitcase, which looked deceptively full. No apologies extended, the dear lady glared at me before moving off, as if I were of no consequence, and in fact, I was bothering her! In hindsight, I thought to myself that I should have left her to sit there and become the joke of the entire train! Meanwhile, the giggles from the back of the train got louder, as my sister, not one to keep quiet, found a common topic to engage the travellers next to her. Very soon, the conservative English people had relaxed considerably, to take in the show of the calamity waiting to happen in our pink lady, as they excitedly chatted away throughout our journey.

In the days to come, I would see more of that vivacious personality of my big sister re-emerge, as she engaged food vendors, store attendants and even the hotel staff where we stayed. Not for the first time, I thought of this strong-willed person who was my sister, who took life full on, afraid of no one regardless of culture or race. As the train rolled on, our pink lady headed to the bathroom, close to where we were sitting, oblivious to the attention which she had attracted. Within moments, we all heard a loud thud coming from the bathroom, and our carriage erupted in laughter. It appeared, that our lady had fallen on the ground! We could not help because she was locked into the bathroom. Soon she exited, looking a bit dishevelled but none the wiser about the attention she was causing. However, no sooner had she exited the bathroom, the train screeched to a halt and before we knew it the poor dear was sprawled on the ground before us, having lost her balance altogether. My husband, got into action immediately and helped her back on her feet. Laughter turned into dismay, as we looked at the poor thing now a little bruised and dusty from the fall. As the train halted, our pink lady briskly alighted, and as we peeped out the window, she hastily made her way down the train station, disappearing into the crowd. I was amazed that she looked absolutely normal and gave no indication of her inebriated state.

By the time we arrived in Coventry, darkness had begun to creep in. But as we made the short drive to the hotel, I wondered about the people in Coventry since on more than one occasion, I witnessed first-hand their love for pubs and drinking. It was not uncommon during my daily treks in the city, to see unruly bunches of people drinking inside and outside the many pubs. Our journey to Coventry, though bumpy, had gotten off on a positive start. There was much excitement and expectations for the much-anticipated graduation ceremony and for our short visit to Coventry. I was more than elated to have my family with me to share this momentous occasion of my life with and to show them this special place in my life.

From London to Paris and Back

During our short few days in London, we were able to take in as many sights as possible but the most memorable was going to the theatre to see 'Lady in Black'. The theatre was rather small and looked cheap inside, and I wondered if we had gotten a raw deal from the booth at the corner of Piccadilly Street, where last minute tickets were bought at a relatively cheap price. I was even more surprised that having got to the theatre late, we were in the front row seats. Before long, I realised why since we had to strain our necks upwards to see the actors performing on the stage.

The play itself was very good but I could not understand why there were so few actors on the set and it became almost a monologue with one actor doing most of the talking. My sister must have been enjoying the play tremendously because she would not stop laughing. In fact, her laughter was so loud in the quiet theatre, that on more than one occasion, I saw our lone actor glare at her angrily for distracting him. After much elbow jabbing from us, she eventually got the message, although that did not stop her muted laughter which went on for a long time.

After a few days, we trekked over to the station which was directly opposite the hotel where we stayed. It was quite a sight to see all of us walking in a row with suitcases dragging behind us as we made our way across the road, into the train station, down the long corridor to the immigration officer. It did not take long for the designated train to arrive and we all excitedly got on, to make our way to Paris. My sister was like a kid going on an excursion for the first time and I thought to myself how nice it was to be taken care of and just enjoy the experience. For my very independent sister, accustomed to being in control, she must have felt very comfortable and secure to relinquish all control to me.

My mother too was very happy, for the first time in her life, she was in Europe and heading to France, a place she probably heard of and glimpsed in the movies she saw on her television from the comfort of her little living room in the country. When we returned to Trinidad, I ensured that I gave her an album of photos from her trip as a keepsake. One day, she mentioned to me how happy she was to see these places which she never thought she would see in her lifetime. She never ceased to tell me about how she recognised the church which we visited in Paris when she was looking at her inspirational channel each morning.

My husband did not show much emotion, perhaps overwhelmed by the large party of females with no male companion to bond with. I think he was very disappointed that my brother-in-law from New York did not make the trip as planned and he was left with us; the lone male among a bunch of headstrong, tempestuous females. He did mention to me that he would not be going on any more family trips after this! This turned out to be untrue since we did make another trip, this time to Orlando with another headstrong sister.

Our trip to Paris was uneventful, however, when we left the station to get to the hotel, which according to the map was close to the station, I realised that I had fallen for the trick of my profession, too good marketing! We were given directions by a cabdriver, who volunteered to walk us to the hotel. Off we all went, with suitcases in hand, in a file, down the street, following this total stranger to find this elusive hotel somewhere in Paris. After about fifteen minutes, we began to wonder if we were being misled by this helpful stranger.

We stopped to ask a gentleman on the pavement for directions and he indicated that the hotel was much further, volunteering to call us a cab instead. Meanwhile, our self-designated guide, seeing what was taking place, intervened and a heated argument ensued between him and the person whom we asked direction from. Although, I did not know much French, I could tell that some bad words were flying back and forth. Our guide was very passionate and vociferous, pointing us to where the hotel was, a short distance away. In exasperation we continued to follow him, and true to form he did lead us to the right place, not five minutes away. We shamefully thanked him and went into the hotel.

The hotel was small and modest but tastefully done, however, the overwhelming dark colours made me wonder if I had chosen a brothel which the French used regularly to play out their amorous nature. If so, we saw no signs of one-night visitors while we were there, and I was thankful for that. I am not sure what we would have done if we came face to face with ladies and gentlemen of the night.

My first day there, did not go as planned since I had greedily wolfed down a pre-packaged sushi roll in London and got a bad case of food poisoning. I was confined to bed for the entire day and my family was left to explore around the hotel on their own. This suited my husband fine, and he and my daughter set off on their own, glad to have a few minutes to themselves.

We also visited the Louvre museum and was able to see many of the famous paintings and sculptures including the Mona Lisa. Like my visit to the Eiffel Tower, this too left much to be desired – a small painting on the wall which could only be seen properly from close proximity. Unfortunately, that was not possible as throngs of mostly Chinese visitors, hugged the space around the painting, unwilling to let anyone through. I always thought Chinese people to be serene and peaceful people but revised my opinion considerably after this episode as I was jostled and pushed by the Chinese invasion. My only regret about this visit was that we had so few hours to visit the museum which needed at least a week to see all its remarkable treasures.

We were scuttling from room to room, trying to take in as much as we could in the short period we were there. After the museum, we went to a small restaurant for lunch and ordered food with names which we did not understand, except for my big sister who was fluent in French and acted as our translator. My sister ordered duck and was not pleased when the bird arrived looking more than a rat with a tail wrapped in foil. I wanted to die with laughter when I saw her expression of disbelief and dismay! My sister was not pleased when she tried to get the young male waiter to attend to her and I swear I heard her mutter some expletives under her breath. I think he was too busy flirting with my teenage daughter and my niece to care and continued to attend to us in a friendly way, indicating to me that he knew my sister was mad at him. My niece and daughter were very flattered by the attentions of the flamboyant, handsome young French man who openly admired them, perhaps not accustomed to such brashness from a stranger. My husband took this all in good spirit, a beer in hand, saying little but watchfully observing everything.

The next day, we took the train to the Notre Dame cathedral which was located close to the famous Seine River.

The visit there was especially for my mother who loved churches and wore a cross on her neck most times, even though she was born into a Hindu family. We next visited the famous Eiffel Tower and as I stared up at this old, rickety, iron structure, I must say that I was not that impressed. I was even less impressed by the number of dark- skinned touts who were aggressively selling souvenirs and other trinkets to visitors to the Tower. I certainly was not expecting this shanty town behaviour in one of the most famous sites in the world.

By the time we had finished visiting the Tower, we sat down in a small café on the side of the street to have a few drinks. We all ordered wines except for my husband who stuck to his beer. The French waiters, mostly young, attractive males were very friendly and my sister flirted mercilessly and shamelessly with them in their native language. By midnight, I hinted to her that it was time to go since the trains may stop working at a certain hour, and unless we wanted to sleep in the café we should leave. We hastily made our way to the waiting train across the road and boarded, thinking how fortunate it was for us to have gotten on the last train. Within five minutes an announcement was made indicating that they had found a suspicious package in the train and we could either wait until it was sorted or we could find alternate transport. It was the biggest hint to get off that train. Within minutes, the train was emptied of all its passengers.

We strolled back to the small café and our waiters, sympathetic to our dilemma, literally hounded down two taxis to take us back to the hotel, saying adieu as if we were life-long friends! Our cabdrivers must have had no speed limit, and in a very short time, we were whisked away down beautifully lit streets which I knew from the unending lights was the famous Champs Elysees. The lights disappeared quickly and soon we were deposited outside our hotel.

The next day, our brief stay in Paris had come to an end and sadly we headed back to the train station, to make the trip back to London. Given the large party, we decided to walk back to the station which we thought was close by. This was a grave mistake since we had forgotten that we had to go up the hilly street with suitcases in hand. We also miscalculated the time to get there and by the time we had arrived, the train had left without us. Our consternation turned to happiness when we were put on the very next train to London within minutes.

The Quaint Hotel
in Edinburgh

Many years after my studies ended, it had become habitual to return to that special place, in the heart of England which I had grown to love. On this particular trip, I decided to visit Scotland via train with my daughter, with a brief stop off at Coventry to see my supervisor and his family.

On that cold September afternoon, we were picked up in front of the hotel and taken to have supper at his home. It was wonderful to meet his lovely family, his twin boys, his wife whom I had gotten to know over the years and his extremely exuberant teenage daughter, who instantly befriended my own daughter. The combination of English and Kenyan food was very delicious after which we sat down to enjoy the rest of the afternoon listening and comparing both Kenyan and Trinidad music on their television. Their music focused on love and the gentle movement of the hips, while ours was mostly on wine and jam with a faster rhythm. My Kenyan hosts did not seem too impressed, although I did see a glint of masculine pleasure registered on my host face as he looked at the bikini-clad female masqueraders dancing suggestively, to our carnival music. His wife must have seen it too because she got up and did a good rendition of a Trini 'wine' for him! I am sure I heard him say quietly that he would be visiting us around the carnival season. I marvelled that our cultures were so different, although I could have discerned some similarities in the beats of the music.

The trip to Edinburgh, Scotland, entailed a brief connection from Birmingham Station and before long we were on the train to Scotland, passing through towns with fancy names such as Elephant and Castle. I could not help but think of J. K. Rowling and how many hours she must have sat in these trains, drawing inspiration from the many train stations which seemed remarkably similar to the ones in the Harry Potter films. I loved the English countryside and ate up the many sites of rolling green plains some with sheep lazily grazing on its lush green meadows. I am not sure if my daughter shared my enthusiasm since she had her headphones on and seemed oblivious to the beautiful scenery as the train meandered lazily on.

When we finally arrived in Edinburgh, I looked for the exits and became confused since the streets appeared to be a floor above. I was relieved when I spied some lifts close to the stairs and hastily made my way to its glass doors. I hailed the first taxi in sight and was elated when the brawny driver indicated that the hotel was very close by. When I asked him if he knew the hotel, he shrugged nonchalantly muttering that it was one of the best hotels in town! It was my first experience of wry Scottish humour since instead of the modern hotel I was expecting, the taxi stopped in front of an old, historic building with a barely visible sign. Hesitantly, I asked if he was sure that this was the right place as he unceremoniously began offloading the suitcases unto the pavement. I was prepared to stay in the taxi thinking it must be a joke. But the driver sped off with a sardonic look on his face, leaving us standing there on the pavement.

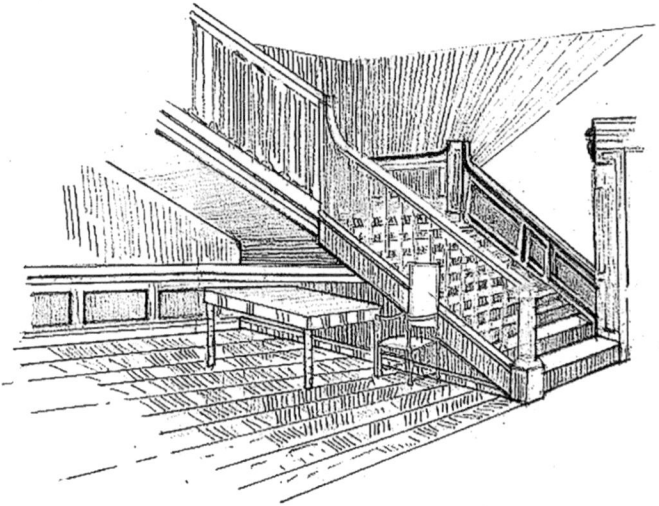

Reluctantly, we made our way in and were greeted by a buxom woman behind a desk in a very narrow corridor, which turned out to be the main lobby. As I admiringly looked up the winding, heavily carpeted wooden stairs which seemed to go on forever; I wondered what I had gotten myself into. Soon I was handed a couple of large keys for a room on the second floor and told at the same time that there were no lifts, since the building was too old to get the approvals to install them! What, no lift, I exclaimed in amazement! Glancing at the deep purple carpet on the winding stairs. "Don't worry," the landlady said. "I will help you," and without batting an eye, lifted one of the suitcases over her head and scampered up the stairs, disappearing out of sight and leaving us there with our mouths wide open. This was no easy feat since my daughter did not learn the art of packing and seemed to have stuffed everything from her bedroom in Trinidad, including five pairs of shoes, into her heavy suitcase. Both my daughter and I looked up in amazement, then gingerly followed behind, grabbing at the banisters, so as not to topple down the winding stairs. An immaculately dressed gentleman, who was descending the stairs, seeing our predicament, offered to assist us, which we gladly accepted. But the landlady was less than honest and the second floor proved to really be the third floor, and given that our suitcases were very heavy, tripped our gallant gentleman a few steps down; his fall only being arrested by our heavy suitcases. He looked at the landlady exasperatedly with flushed cheeks and did not offer to help a second time; marching off without looking back. I tried very hard to suppress the laughter threatening to burst from me in seconds, even though I was grateful for his help.

Finally, when we got to our rooms, we were pleasantly surprised since the rooms were huge, although the colours were in deep purple and had a very austere look, like something out of the horror movie 'Dark Shadows'. We also had three beds and a window which overlooked the back of the building. My daughter was elated as she tested each bed and soon like any other kid, jumped on the bed to peep out the window and take in the awesome sight before us. From that height, we were able to see the chimney tops of high- roofed buildings leading to the glimmer of waters in the ocean, way off in the distance. But our glee was short-lived, as we discovered that our small bathroom window which was wide open, was stuck and no amount of yanking would pull the wooden shutters down. Very soon, a young man entered to fix the problem. Without complaining, he got to it, giving it a good yank until the shutters rolled down and I could tell that this was nothing out of the ordinary for him. I could not help but tell him that I liked the hotel as he was about to leave, and knowing that I was teasing, said a very expressionless but sardonic, "Good Night."

But our quaint hotel had some more surprises in store for us. The following morning while blow-drying my damp hair, I was startled to hear 'pop, pop' and a sizzling sound followed by the smell of something burning; only to discover that the hotel's blow-dryer had exploded in my hands! Five minutes later, I heard a rap on my door and without batting an eye, the landlady handed me a replacement, indicating that I should leave the last one in a drawer! By this time, I could not contain myself anymore as I fell back unto the bed rolling with uncontrollable laughter. But our hotel experience did not end there, the advertised free breakfast turned out to be a motley of cold meats and a barely there salad! For those who got in late without dinner and were famished in the morning; this turned out to be a big disappointment. The food was served by a couple of silent, young male waiters who made a great deal of looking busy so as not to engage the silently, angry breakfast contingent, in the small room. My daughter and I did all that we could not to burst out in fits of giggles when we went to the breakfast room each morning.

Having visited Scotland before, I was excited to show my daughter the beautiful old city which led to the famous Edinburgh Castle at the top of the hill or Castle Rock. I recalled on my first visit there, years ago, arriving late in the night and being whisked past the castle dramatically perched on the cliff's edge as if suspended from air. It was a sight that never left my mind. After breakfast, we headed to the main street, less than ten-minute walk from where we stayed. Within minutes, our eyes fell on the miles of ancient buildings lined up perfectly in a row and forming a dramatic silhouette against the blue skies. Even though, this was my second visit, I still gasped in awe at the stunning picture of ancient turrets above the equally ancient buildings stretching as far as the eyes could see, ending with the castle perched on top of a hill, which I only too remembered. I looked at my daughter who seemed just as amazed as I was as we stood silently looking at the picturesque buildings before us. Excitedly we made our way toward the buildings, first down some narrow streets and up some small lanes which left us breathless as we climbed towards the castle. I had forgotten how steep the climb was and foolishly kept my heeled boots on making the trek even more difficult. My daughter had on sneakers and walked energetically ahead of me, glancing over her shoulders occasionally, to make sure that I was following.

Abruptly, our lane ended and we found ourselves in one of the busiest streets in Edinburgh, the famous Royal Mile road, which went up and down lined with all types of shops one can imagine, including pubs with loud patrons drinking pints of beers. It reminded me of Harry Potter's first discovery of Diagon Alley in The Sorcerer's Stone. We spent the entire day, walking up and down that wobbly street, looking at the many trinkets and other goods on display in those small shops that I loved so much. I was enthralled to see a gentleman fully garbed in traditional kilted wear playing the bagpipe on one of the narrow streets. As we paused to listen to him, I thought how hauntingly ethereal and light the music was. The tour of the castle could not be completed without a cup of tea in one of the tea rooms.

On our way back to the hotel, we were fortunate to see a live band perform. As I listened to the music, my eyes surveyed the enthusiastic street crowd against the backdrop of these ancient buildings, thinking how fortunate we were to have such a wonderful experience.

The Floating City of Venice

Over the years, my frequent visits to Coventry gave me the confidence to explore other parts of Europe such as Venice in Italy. Venice did not fascinate me alone, for centuries many men and women have immortalised this beautiful city in paintings, movies and books. I have always likened it to the fabled city of Atlantis which disappeared without a trace and continues to haunt scientists and explorers as demonstrated in the number of documentaries on all sorts of theories ranging from conspiracy, natural disasters, and diseases to alien theory, which are available for the questioning and curious mind. Much later, when I visited the British museum in the heart of London, I marvelled at the care and precision which some famous painters of the medieval period took in painting images of wooden ships with their voluminous sails attached to huge masts, gently sailing in the beautiful waters of the Aegean Sea and of terracotta-coloured buildings, piled high on top of each other as if suspended in the still blue waters surrounded by small, curved wooden boats floating idly close by. When I did visit, I was in awe of these gondolas steered by handsome, olive-coloured Venetian men, which glided lazily in the city's watery roads. More so, when I saw how they seemed to be almost submerged in the choppy, aqua-marine waters of the lagoon, I became fearful and refused to sit in them. No amount of coaxing by my daughter, who had accompanied me there, got me to board one of these famous vessels. Not one to tempt fate, the fear of a watery death so far from home, kept me rooted on firm land.

As a student of history, I was aware of the fabled Venetian sailors who sailed from this port next to St Mark's Square, around the world, looking for gold, spices and other precious items which they used to bargain and trade during the Byzantine period. They were part of that era when the Turks held the balance of power in their hands and cut new trading routes around the world looking for precious gold and other items of trade, from foreign lands to enrichen their already burgeoning empire, grown fat from the ill-gotten largesse, from far off places. I wondered at the brevity of these adventurous souls, sailing across those blue, treacherous waters, during this historic period of time, so that they could please their wealthy and powerful benefactor. This could be seen in the ostentatious use of gold in the Doge's Palace overlooking the port. I have never seen an entire palace built of marble as well as ceilings of pure gold together with staircases stitched with intricate patterns lined with gold, leading to the top floor where the Doge or emperor had his private quarters. As I breathlessly climbed those steep steps, I thought that the Doge must have been in remarkably good health, to be able to climb those steep stairs several times every day. I also walked through spectacular official meeting rooms with grand stages decorated with beautiful, intricate wooden patterns.

The famous Marco Polo was a colourful character of that time, attired in his voluminous clothing and tasselled hat as he commandeered his men to chase after places and people in far off lands. Living in the twenty-first century, it is difficult to imagine that era of bygone days when the main profession was trading and the main form of transport was via the sea. Apart from the few of us who study or read history, it is difficult to fathom that the richest and most famous parts of the world and the most powerful people resided in the Mediterranean. I often wondered if the idea of setting up a caliphate being pursued by ISIS, is an attempt to capture this bygone era of Islamic supremacy in the modern word. As a child of the Caribbean, our history education usually began with that famous discovery of our land, the Spanish sailor Christopher Columbus who sailed across the Atlantic with three boats, the Niña, the Pinta and the Santa Maria in search of gold, to please his insatiable Spanish monarch, in their quest to be richest superpowers in the world. It is written that this gentleman was deeply influenced by the legendary Marco Polo and it always amused me that he must have been the worst sailor of the seas at that time since he was really looking for India and took the wrong direction and instead of heading east, sailed in a westerly direction. It was pure coincidence that he stumbled upon the islands in the Caribbean and foolishly thought that he was in India and christened us 'The West Indies'.

As I read more about the history of Trinidad, I grew wary of that claim by the Spaniards that they first discovered this island since there were thousands of indigenous peoples who lived here for centuries when he came here. Even more disturbing was the fact that most of these people were exploited and eventually wiped out under that rubric term 'conquered' and even more disturbing, it was done in the name of Christendom. I cannot fathom that the peace-loving Jesus would have had anything to do with the wiping out of millions of indigenous people in his name. As more Caribbean people have begun to interrogate our history, this anomaly is being corrected in our contemporary history books; though I fear that it will take a much longer time to correct this misconception and biased view of history, created by European writers in the minds of readers.

It was not mere coincidence that I decided to venture outside the traditional tourist destinations and visit this city nestled in the Mediterranean Sea on one of my visits to England. No easy feat when one considered the nine-hour flight, over the Atlantic Ocean to London. Our trip started off a bit bumpy since our passports expired a few days shy of the stipulated three-month requirement for visiting Italy. I was aghast when I tried to check in online 24 hours before the flight to discover a note telling me that I did not have sufficient documents. At first, I thought it was a computer glitz and almost ignored it but good sense prevailed and when I opened the note, I started to panic. In a frenzy, I called the airline's customer service office and was told that the only way I could enter Venice is if they called immigration and they allowed it; adding that this was highly unlikely. As I sat in my daughter's room, I looked at her attempt at brevity and decided to seek the assistance of our consulate in London. But alas, they were all on the long Easter break and no one picked up the phone. As I sat there, I called back the airline, explaining my predicament, volunteering to immediately go down to the airport to resolve the problem before the morning flight. I was elated when the person agreed and my daughter and I quickly journeyed to London City Airport, across from North Greenwich. As luck would have it, the helpful customer service officer called the Venetian Immigration, only to discover that the person on the other end could not speak English. Luckily, for us, his female colleague sitting next to him was Italian. She must have seen our desperate faces and overheard our conversation because without hesitating she took the phone, speaking authoritatively with her fellow men in Italy. We were so relieved when at the end of the conversation, a note was added to our passports, giving us access to the country. As we left the airline, I looked at my daughter, telling her that she must always have faith in the universe, even when nothing seems to be going right. Suddenly, the world had become happy again and we were ready to travel the next morning to Venice.

The famous Rialto Bridge

As we entered Venice, I was determined to experience this famous Italian city to its fullest and headed to the waterfront to get the water bus to make the short journey. When we finally arrived at the port, our brief walk was cut short by a very dashing looking gentleman, asking if we would like to take a water taxi to our destination instead. As I stared into his handsome face, which I am sure I must have seen on a poster somewhere, I heard myself saying yes, in spite of the pricy fare. He must have been a race-car driver because as the engine started, I saw waves of water kicking up angrily behind us, as we raced between large wooden stilts rammed deep into the water on two sides, creating a natural water road towards beautiful, outlined buildings some distance away. As we scrambled to the covered part of the boat, fearful that we had chosen badly, I sardonically asked the driver if he liked to race; smiling mischievously, he nodded in the affirmative, perhaps having fun at our expense.

It was a good decision to take his cab because it was the best introduction to the city. From the hood of the boat, we got a spectacular view of the city spread out in the waters of the blue lagoon. I felt like the painting which I saw in one of the museums I visited had just come alive! The white dome-shaped buildings seemed like they were floating in the air, and I felt that I had just been transported to an ephemeral city in the sky. As my eyes travelled downwards, I saw the thick concrete buildings firmly planted in the blue waters, as if to remind me that I was still on earth. As we passed under the arched walkway of the famous Rialto Bridge, I marvelled at the beautiful architecture of the buildings alongside the rivulets, painted in all hues of pastels and terracotta, with small shuttered windows, looking out to sea. There was an order, serenity and peacefulness about these buildings with the ocean which surrounded them. I only wished, that in time, my own country would have a deeper appreciation of the aesthetics of blending our natural landscape into our housing developments.

As the boat glided through narrow lanes, I got a closer look at the buildings and water surrounding them. The water was dark and green, and in some places the putrid smell of urine assaulted by nostrils, making me hold my breath, as we slowly moseyed along the meandering river courses. Up close, the buildings seemed older and I could see the moss with some small shellfish clinging to these ancient buildings just above the still water. As the driver gently manoeuvred the boat so as not to bump into the tourist laden gondolas, steered by handsome men attired in striped black and white attire, I was taken aback by the maze of unending buildings and narrow cobbled streets with its traffic of busy tourists, walking frenetically from place to place. Feeling like I had just entered the hobbit's realm, I looked up to see an outstretched hand being offered to me to exit the boat.

Although, the hotel which was perched on the water's edge seemed unimpressive from the outside, once inside, there was an easy earthiness and charm to its terracotta painted walls and glassed covered gazebo in the centre of the hotel, which doubled up as the main breakfast area in the mornings and transformed into a romantic, dimly lit restaurant in the night. As the bellman led us to our bedroom, down a narrow corridor, I looked up to see rays of sunlight peeping through small windows, illuminating the dark corridor with natural light. When he opened our bedroom, I thought I had stepped into an art gallery. Everything was porcelain white, lined with silver and white Byzantine motifs including a complete marble bathroom and mirrored corridors. In the middle of the large spacious room was a magnificent queen-sized bed big enough to fit more than two persons. It seemed like this room was fitted for royalty as we gingerly made our way in, not wanting to touch anything for fear of spoiling the immaculate décor. So far, this was a good introduction to Venice.

Wanting to continue our euphoric experience, we decided to have a sumptuous dinner in the main restaurant. As we entered the restaurant, I could not believe that the practical area I saw earlier on my way to my room had been transformed into the most romantic restaurant I had ever seen with dimly lit candles placed on table tops. As we were ushered to our table, I could not help but stare at the elegant patrons, sipping their wines in large, long-stemmed glass goblets, chatting happily while eating their dinner. As I looked up at the glass-covered roof, I realised that there were vines snaking lazily across the gazebo illuminated by the dim lights of the bedrooms surrounding the restaurant. The meal was perfection! The four-course meal comprised an assortment of Italian breads served with olive oil, prosciutto and cheese, followed by lamb and potatoes, a dessert of pancetta and gelato, washed down with a glass of fine Italian wine. As we made our way back to our room, I thought that in spite of the challenges of getting there, it was worth the effort.

We awoke early the next morning to the sounds of raindrops beating down noisily on the roof of the hotel and soon discovered that the weather was dismally cold outside. It did not deter us and soon after breakfast we headed off to explore the small city and find the famous St Mark's Square. Propelled by the large steeple which seemed not to far from us, we headed out the hotel, down the narrow alley, lined by famous brand name shops and restaurants with small tables and chairs tightly placed just outside their doors. As we briskly walked by, my eyes caught the intricate patterns of a beautiful green, Venetian rug displayed in a small shop. As I entered the shop, I could hear the melodious sound of Italian music in the background. It was all so beautiful! Who would have thought to pair an antique shop with its rustic décor and musty scents with the most sensuous music I have ever heard.

As quickly as I entered, I exited, not wanting to waste too much time in one place with so much to see in this famous city. By this time, the city had awoken and in spite of the biting cold, the narrow streets became filled with hustling tourists and patrons heading in the same direction. Instinctively, we followed the lines of people and suddenly found ourselves in a large open space surrounded by equally large Romanesque, square-shaped, columned buildings, lining the circumference of the area. The famous St Mark's square was dotted with some historical buildings, including the St Mark's Basilica which I decided to explore another day. Within the Square were a number of restaurants with tables and chairs placed strategically outside each restaurant and attended by immaculately dressed male waiters. Some of the restaurants had small musical bands playing soft music to attract patrons.

Glimpsing the green water of the lagoon at the far end of the Square, we decided to head in that direction to get a closer look. As we drew closer to the water, my eyes were mesmerised by the picture-perfect landscape of white Roman-styled buildings with its round rotundas almost floating in the air against the background of overcast blue skies across the waters. Although for centuries, many artists have tried to capture this picture in their artwork, none have been able to truly depict the astounding beauty in front of us. As we headed down the lane on the water's edge, I took in the serenity of the archaic and historical Italian buildings, with its shuttered windows gracefully overlooking the lagoon. In front of the buildings were numerous tourist booths, selling all types of souvenirs such as laced umbrellas and fans, wire masks and large scarves with Venetian prints on them. But the most interesting to me were the many original landscape paintings displayed by the many street artists and sold for small sums.

Being a large connoisseur of street paintings, I quickly purchased two to add to my collection. Today, it sits proudly in my office with the rest of my collection.

The following day, we visited the St Mark's Basilica which was unnaturally dark inside and seemed to be a cross between a mosque and a church. In my own country, known for its diverse religions and many mosques, churches and temples; this fusion of a mosque and church left me slightly disturbed. The unnatural quiet and heaviness of the cathedral seemed a more fitting home for vampires rather than monks and priests, I thought to myself as we tiptoed quietly around, afraid to make a sound. As we waited for the guide to take us around, I stared up at the dark, green and gold etched domes, above my head and dimly lit lamps hanging from the ceiling, at the same time inhaling the deep, musty smell of incense and centuries of antiquity oozing from its concrete walls. If I had met the oldest woman in the planet – the Eiffel Tower in Paris; I had just met the oldest man – in Venice! Both relics of a bygone era, defying time to stand firm as a witness to the future.

I felt like this too was like a maze with small, dwarf-sized rooms in corners, leading to, I am not sure where. I wondered how many secrets did this cathedral hold; how many men with bloodied hands sat before the hallowed figures of Jesus and Mary, and begged them to have mercy on their wretched souls; how many widowed wives' tears wetted the pews as they cried for husbands lost at sea or killed in wars; how many births, funerals and weddings did it bear witness to with the passing of time and changing of seasons. After what seemed to be an insurmountable time, I was glad the tour had ended and to leave the cathedral and drink in the cool air outside to clear my heavy head and soothe my disturbed senses. I am not sure what the Venetians were trying to achieve with this cathedral, but although I felt drawn into its bosom like a moth to the light; I was compelled to flee from its smothering darkness.

Over the few days we were there, we explored buildings, visited museums and learnt about the interesting history of this famous city. Even though the city was small and attracts thousands of tourists daily, I found that it maintained its quaint charm and mystery. In 2018, I was saddened to learn that this beautiful place was completely flooded with more than four feet of water in some places. I have a hunch that in time to come, this famous city which is surrounded with water like Atlantis, would disappear from the landscape, remembered in tales told in story books.

The End of the Journey and New Beginnings

I vividly remember on that cold winter day on December 12 of 2012, sitting nervously in the waiting room to be taken to my examination or better known as viva in academic language, in an adjacent building. I had made the last leg of my academic journey to Coventry to prepare for my oral examination. I was reliably informed that my thesis had been sent to the internal and external examiners and that the date for my examination was all set for this fortuitous date in the calendar. During the short period I was there, I stayed in the little hotel, which I had grown to love at the bottom of the street, not far from the university and St Michaels Cathedral. Each day, I would sit on my bed reading and rereading my thesis, trying to think of every possible question which should come my way. The university had also prepared me well since each year I had to go through a similar exercise with a large panel of senior academics. I was also put through two mock vivas to fully prepare me for the examination, so that by the time my examination came around I was more than prepared for it.

On that momentous day, time seemed to stand still as I robotically went through my activities and made my way to the designated office to be escorted to the examination room. As I entered the room, I was surprised to see a lone academic sitting there and I soon found myself shaking the hands of my external examiner. He told me I did a good piece of work which put me at ease immediately. Soon after, another gentleman walked past us and he too introduced himself as the internal examiner. Very soon, they were escorted out the building to the examination room. My early introductions to these two academics did not ease my fear and I could barely feel my legs beneath me as I was led quietly to the long building where my panel eagerly awaited me.

It seemed like an eternity before I was called in together with my supervisor to the examination room. My lost confidence soon returned as I was interrogated for about one hour about the pages of research I had done and my nervousness gradually subsided. Before long, I was asked to sit outside, while they deliberated on my results. There was a deadly silence around me and perhaps only my laboured breathing gave away my agitated state of mind as I sat silently in the waiting room with my supervisor.

When I was called back in for my results, like a prisoner on death sentence, I stood before them, hoping for the best but fearing the worst. My nervousness quickly evaporated as my mind registered the great news that I had passed my examination and that they were very impressed with the extensive research which I had conducted, over the time of my study. My years of hard work and sacrifice had paid off handsomely and I knew that my life would never be the same again. In celebration of my achievement, I was invited to lunch with both gentlemen together with my director of studies in the faculty eating room. I could barely remember the conversation or what I ate as I sat before them in a trance like state trying to comprehend that I had just achieved a tremendous milestone in my life. By the time the lunch had finished, reality started to set in and I could not wait to share my good news with my local supervisor and family abroad. I knew that they were all just as anxious and nervous for me. When I broke the news, I could feel their sense of relief and tremendous joy for my achievement in Trinidad and I was excited to return home to celebrate with them.

I was very touched when my supervisor, Dr Fred Mudhai, accompanied me to the hotel and spent a few minutes discussing the comments from the examiners. I knew he was anxious for me and was just as relieved and happy at the outcome of the examination. Knowing that I was alone in

England, he graciously invited me to his home and I was moved when I realised that his family had planned a small celebration to commemorate this momentous day. To this day, I still look back fondly at all the times I have spent with him and his family who embraced me as part of their own. To this day, Fred and his family continue to be some of my close and dearest friends.

The very next day, I was booked on a flight to return to Trinidad and to resume my working life at The University of the West Indies. But my journey into academic life had only just begun. Soon after returning to work, I decided to test the waters and submitted my thesis for publication by UWI Press. I was elated when I got an immediate response indicating their interest in publishing my research into a book. However, my elation soon dissipated when I was told the extent of work which needed to be done to get the research ready for publication. I was optimistic enough to think that this process was an easy one. I soon found out that this journey would take me to another level of academic consciousness. Convinced about the relevance of my topic and determined to put my research out to the wider public, I got down to the business of writing my book. I soon discovered the joy of academic writing and attacked this project with much gusto and enjoyment. On 14 September, 2017, I launched my book, *Mediatized Political Campaigns: A Caribbean Perspective* at the Institute of Critical Thinking at The University of the West Indies, where my journey had started. It was also my first opportunity to share a stage with the former campus principal and Pro-vice-chancellor for Planning, Dr Bhoendradatt Tewarie who was also my local supervisor.

During this period, my daughter who attended St. Augustine Girls High School, won an open scholarship in Languages which gave her the added advantage of studying abroad. I was elated when she decided to pursue her undergraduate degree in England. Although, she did not choose Coventry University as I did, I was happy that she was accepted in her university of choice: Goldsmiths University in London. I do believe my positive experiences in Coventry and the resulting success which I achieved, motivated her to follow in my footsteps. Over the years, I had primed her for her study abroad experience, knowing how beneficial it would be to her own growth and development; living, studying in a different society and interacting with international students. I was not to be disappointed as I saw her develop into a strong, independent, young woman. Over the years I was there, she visited once and I was happy to introduce her to dorm life since she stayed in the small apartment which I occupied. Her induction to university life and the UK was deliberate, so that when the time came for her to choose a country to study, England was the natural choice. When she attended my graduation in Coventry, I think it made her realise that she too could live out her dream as I did.

Over the last few years, I have said countless tearful goodbyes to my daughter in the airport as she prepared to board her flight to England. It never gets easy and I do not suppose it ever would. But my hope is that she draws inspiration from the life I have lived, with the hope that she would surpass all that I have achieved and take her rightful place in the universe. I have had tremendous support from family, friends and those near and dear to my heart. I have made good friends in Coventry and I continue to journey there occasionally to reconnect with them or simply bask in the ambience of that peaceful environment. Although, I knew that I had come to the end of my academic journey in Coventry and I would miss this place and the friends I made along the way, I was fortunate to maintain a relationship with the university and would return there for an official visit to Coventry Technology Park. I was elated that The University of the West Indies also entered into a formal relationship with Coventry University.

Launch of my book *Mediatized Political Campaigns: A Caribbean Perspective*, on September 14 2017, at the Institute of Critical Thinking, The University of the West Indies, St. Augustine Campus

Platform party: Mr Andy Johnson, journalist and former CEO Government Information Services; Professor Patricia Mohammed, director graduate studies and research, UWI; Professor Densil Williams, pro vice chancellor, University Office of Planning; author (Indrani Bachan-Persad); and Dr. Bhoendradatt Tewarie, member of parliament and former pro vice chancellor and campus principal, St. Augustine Campus.

Author with family: Chelsea (daughter), Kassinath (husband) and Poptee Bachan (mother).